CHAMPIONSHIP BASEBALL

HANK BAUER

Championship
BASEBALL

DOUBLEDAY & COMPANY, INC., GARDEN CITY, NEW YORK

1968

To my beloved wife, Charlene

ACKNOWLEDGMENTS

I wish to acknowledge the assistance of my friend Bob Smith for putting this book into readable shape.

I gratefully acknowledge the contribution to this book made by Louis Requena, who took the photographs.

CONTENTS

What Makes a Good Ballplayer   *1*

The Catcher   *7*

The Pitcher   *25*

The First Baseman   *41*

Playing the Infield   *49*

The Second Baseman   *59*

The Shortstop   *61*

The Third Baseman   *65*

Playing the Outfield   *71*

Hitting   *79*

Base Running   *95*

Winning Ball Games   *111*

WHAT MAKES A GOOD BALLPLAYER

I do not profess to be any great baseball strategist. I am no John McGraw, nor even Leo Durocher. I don't sit up nights working out schemes for building runs without base hits or for outwitting the enemy with a new combination play. What I am I guess is a hunch manager. If I get a feeling that a certain play might work—a hit-and-run, a double steal—why, I'll send out the sign for it. Then if it works, I'm a genius. If it doesn't, I'll take the blame.

These hunches are really hunches. They are not the result of any long strategy meeting before the game or of some mental blueprint that I have kept stored in my skull. But I suppose, if anyone was to analyze them, it would turn out that the hunches probably do have some basis in observation. Lots of times, you will pick up the notion that a pitcher is going to go to first base on the next pitch, and you won't even know where the notion came from. But in all likelihood, there is some little gesture, or small shift in position that you have observed unconsciously that is giving the move away. So I suppose my long years of watching baseball players helps me with my hunches. But I still cannot lay out for you any secret system for winning ball games without good ballplayers.

My idea of a good ballplayer is a team player. Baseball is a team game, and not a test of individual strength and skill. One thing I insist on with my boys—and believe me I am no Svengali and no slave driver—is a readiness to forget individual records for the sake of bringing the ball club in first. If we get a man on second base with nobody out, and a single run is valuable, I am going to ask the batter to hit to right and put that man on third. And I don't care who the batter is or what his chances are of posting the highest average in the league. If he is not ready to sacrifice a time at bat for the sake of the club, then he does not belong on my team.

I do not undertake to teach baseball to my ballplayers either, although I can recognize a ballplayer who knows his business. I have played every position there is to play on a ball diamond and at least understand what each man should be trying to do. But I know that every ballplayer has his own way of doing things and I don't insist that he try to do them my way. By the time he gets to the big leagues, he should know his business anyway. There were at least two ballplayers on my championship club who knew more baseball than I did. They were Frank Robinson and Luis Aparicio. I depended on Luis especially, to help move the outfielders around. And I know Frank Robinson can give me lessons in handling a bat.

I don't mean that the coaches and I don't find fault, don't watch the players on the field and at bat to pick up any weaknesses. We do. We will watch our pitchers, for instance, particularly in the spring, to make sure they are throwing naturally, with the full strength and full length of the arm—that they are not favoring a sore toe or a bum knee or some other injury they may not have told us about or may not even be aware of. We always made it a special point to give our hitters hours of bunting practice—because team play must include bunting. And we will let a man know if he has started to move his head at the plate and is forgetting to watch the ball all the way.

Our strategy might seem pretty elementary to some experts. We have one meeting a year on each club, to go over the batters and appraise their strength in every department. We don't go in for long pre-game huddles after that and I absolutely avoid any public fault-finding. The effort on the diamond is a team effort. But the fault-finding is strictly individual. If some guy has not been putting out as I know he could and should, I will get him alone and find out what's eating him. If a pitcher has been getting a little control-happy and has not been putting his back into his fast ball, there will be no yelling at him on the bench. We'll discuss it man to man where the rest of the club cannot overhear. Even if a man is obviously jaking it, or is putting on the sulks, or putting his own average ahead of the ball club, I will still try to straighten him out in private. It is the way I like to be treated and I think it is one way to hold the player's respect.

I think most of the ballplayers on my club do respect me and it is important to the morale of the team that they do. Some of this "respect," especially on the part of the younger players, may be laid to the reputation the sportswriters have so generously built for me—the reputation of being a really tough bird who is likely to tee off on anyone who gets in his way. Just between you and me, nothing could be farther from the truth. I am no professional hard guy at all. I have complete control of my temper and probably would rate as a soft touch if I did not work at maintaining my tough-guy reputation. I do that simply by not becoming too buddy-buddy with the ballplayers.

But I don't go in for the bullying and hide-scraping that some old-time managers made their reputation on. That is just not part of my nature. Of course, if some batter forgets to run out a dropped third strike, or just gives a half-hearted stab at beating out a ground ball, I may blow my top to the extent of saying "What the hell goes on here!" But there'll be no recriminations or name-calling. On the ball field, we are all part of the same club. We don't fight each other. We fight the opposition.

We do have discipline, however. When a club is playing together, when they respect each other and respect the manager—and especially if they are winning ball games, discipline is fairly easy to enforce. Nobody wants to be guilty of letting the team down by allowing himself to get out of playing shape. So it usually takes no more than an occasional reminder —on rare occasions a sharp word and a fine, and often just a hard look, to get a stray back into the fold. And the coaches and I provide daily workouts guaranteed to keep a player's wind strong and his arms and legs limber. The pitchers especially are expected to run, run, and run, except on the day they are slated to pitch, or on the day immediately following. We make them do sprints until the sweat really rolls—not just jogging around the warming track but good hard wind-sprints that require them to put out all the speed they own. We give a lot of attention to our pitchers, keep them in better shape, and move them in and out a lot faster than some clubs seem to.

I hear people say that we have "too many" pitchers, or at least "too many" bullpen pitchers. But I disagree. We have an especially strong bullpen, with some of the best relief pitchers in the game, and this gives us a lot more freedom in making pitching changes. It also permits our young starters to pour on the juice every instant, knowing that, if they do tire, there is plenty of help on hand.

It is natural for the pitcher to want to chalk up a win every time he starts. Any pitcher who takes the mound in the beginning of a ball game thinks of the game as his and will be unhappy if he is taken out, for whatever reason. We have one or two pitchers who really get red in the neck when I lift them. I don't blame them for that. But neither do I give in to them. With us, the club comes first in all things and we expect our pitchers even to pass up a chance to notch another "W" when a change seems necessary. Of course, if we can get nine innings of effective work out of a pitcher, that's what we want. But if one of our lads begins to wobble, or if his good pitch is not working for him, I don't wait around too long before sitting him down. This makes our pitching a whole lot tougher. When an opposition batter has a 3 and 0 count, he is likely to see almost any kind of pitch. In my playing days, a fast ball was almost certain on 3 and 0. But when you bat against the Birds, you can't count on any such thing. The 3 and 0 pitch can be a curve, a slider, a screwball, even a change of pace. We want our pitchers to keep challenging the hitters on every pitch and to give out without fretting over how many innings they still have to go. This is part of our general aggressiveness, which carries into every part of our game.

Aggressive baseball was Casey Stengel's byword, too, and I am not ashamed to admit I learned some of its fine points at the knee of the old Master. I urge our hitters, just as Casey used to urge us, to begin to think hitting and baserunning while they are in the on-deck circle. This is the time for them to check over all the signs in their minds, so they can make sure they know just what the coach means when he flashes them—how they exchange the hit-and-run sign with the runner, and what the chances are of the play's being put on. They can look over the outfielders, make note of where they play in relation to the foul lines and the fences, and recall what they know about their abilities, particularly their throwing ability. They can study the infielders and consider whether they may be called on to bunt—and if so which man may field the ball. They can study the pitcher—and the catcher!—to see what the favorite pitching pattern may be. In short, they begin right away to figure how to get on base, what to do when they get there, and how they can carry out whatever orders the bench may send up. There are many different possibilities in every situation—the man at bat may be on first when the on-deck man comes up. He may hit a double and be on second, with no one out. A ball may then go to right field, where the fielder is not noted for his throwing ability. So perhaps the runner may try to score. What will the batter do then? Try for second to draw the throw and make it certain that we at least have a man on third? Play it safe? Check the third-base coach to see if he is sending the runner in? All these possibilities should be considered as the batter waits his turn.

Even the men on the bench are going to be watching the pitcher, especially with a runner on base, to see if they can figure out the pitcher's move in advance. Or they may study the infielders, to see if they cheat toward the bag on a curve ball—or whatever. We want them all to keep right up to the minute on the play, to know the outs, the count on the batter, the score, the position of the fielders. Everybody has to be in the ball game all the time, whether he's hitting, running, fielding, or just watching. Our speed boys pay particular attention to the pitchers, and even while they sit on the bench they can be getting imaginary starts on the pitcher's motion. We are all of us out to beat the opposition any way we can and everybody works at it full time.

When you play the kind of baseball we do, you can't say any one player is more important than the next. Pitching of course is probably number one in importance. But without strong fielding, your pitching is not going to hold up. Next to pitching is hitting. But everybody can accomplish something at the bat, even if he can't break up a ball game the way the Robbie boys often do. Our own coaching system, is, as I said, strong on bunting. Anybody in our lineup can come through with a bunt when we need one, and we are not a bit ashamed of using bunts to move runners or build up leads. Everybody must know how to move on the bases too. Pure speed is nowhere near as important as knowing how to get a jump, what sort of lead to take, and when to *stop*. We are all for grabbing the extra base. But we don't want men taking wild chances for small gain, so every man has to be aware at all times whether he represents a tying or winning run, and what it may cost the club if he tries for third and gets caught at it.

So I am not singling out any one player as most important when I say that catching is perhaps the biggest job on the club. It requires brains, agility, strength, lots of confidence, an aggressive spirit, and plenty of baseball knowledge. I have been lucky enough to have worked with some of the best catchers in the business, and what advice I give will largely be based on what I learned from watching these men in action or listening to them as they instructed young players in the basics.

Believe me, no one knows better than I that every player has his own way of doing things, at bat or in the field. What is good for one man may not work for the next. But there are certain fundamental requirements that apply to each job in baseball, and those need to be understood before you can discover the way that is best for you to get the job done. If I seem to favor certain styles, methods, or equipment it will just be because some players I have known and admired have favored them. And if I forget to keep saying it, remember that in just about every position, that advice applies—find out the method that is most comfortable and natural for you, and then stick to that.

In every job in baseball, however, you have to learn two things—how to bend your knees and bend your back. In fielding, in pitching, in catching, in batting, in baserunning, you cannot play stiff and straight. Yet I see kids all the time who try to field ground balls with a straight back or without bending the knees. I see young pitchers who move like stiff-legged dolls; batters who try to bunt a low pitch by just lowering the bat; outfielders who jog along on their heels; and even catchers who seem afraid to get down and block a low pitch. So that's a piece of general advice that goes for everybody who wants to play baseball in any position—learn to bend your knees and bend your back. Don't be afraid of the dirt.

THE CATCHER

I've already said something about the skills a fellow needs to be a catcher. There is no doubt in my mind that brains and confidence come first. A catcher has to react in a flash to moves on the bases, has to outguess the batter (and the opposing manager), has to pick up telltale moves that may indicate the hit-and-run, has to keep a catalog of hitters' strengths and weaknesses in his head, and has to know his pitcher well enough to think right along with him, to keep his confidence high, and to detect the first sign of weakening. On top of this he has to have the confidence to act in a split second on his decision.

It should be clear then that to be a successful catcher you need to be a whole lot of baseball player. You have to know just about everything there is to know about the game—what sort of moves to expect from baserunners in all sorts of situations, all the possibilities of a bunt attempt, and everything that might follow from any sort of hit or throw. Because the catcher, having the whole club in front of him, is practically a defensive manager on the field. (And many managers, including me, have done at least a lick of catching.) Naturally you don't pick up all this knowledge from books or from coaching. You get it largely by playing baseball—and by watching the play closely when you are not involved.

As for physical qualifications, you need to have a strong arm, an ability to get rid of the ball in a hurry, and the agility to move swiftly out of your position to throw out a runner, stop a bad pitch, field a bunt, or back up a base. And of course, as I said, you have to flex your knees and bend your back when the occasion demands. A catcher works frequently in a crouch and sometimes on his knees, so a man who cannot squat down easily and stay in that position for long periods without cramping up is never going to be a catcher. Long, lean-muscled legs are probably best. But many catchers have been heavily muscled in the legs. As a matter of fact, Yogi Berra, who developed tremendous leg muscles playing soccer, had such development in his thighs that he could not get down far enough to bring thigh and calf together, and so sometimes they were able to steal his signals from the enemy bench. But Yogi was not musclebound. He could scamper out of that position as well as anyone and had twice as much speed as you ever would have guessed. It is true that many catchers have been fairly slow runners. But the good ones have all been agile, able to unwind themselves in a hurry and quick to slide right or left, or to pounce out over the plate to grab a bunt before it stopped sizzling.

Naturally, the first job a catcher has to learn is to catch the ball, or if he can't catch it at least to stop it. A catcher receives the pitch in one hand. That is, he lets the ball come into his glove and then smothers it with his bare hand and holds it there. He does not extend his bare hand toward the pitch, or let's say he does not do that after once having taken a foul tip on the end of his finger. So his glove is all-important.

There are two kinds of catcher's gloves—the break-rim glove and the solid-rim glove. The break-rim may have one or two "breaks" in the outside edge of the glove to make it easier to fold the glove over the ball. The solid-rim glove does not fold easily. The glove that can be folded quickly makes it easier for you to do your work with one hand, but it does have a drawback. With this glove, you do sometimes get in the habit of grabbing a pitch from on top—bringing the glove down on it, that is, so that you sometimes take a low pitch right out of the strike zone. But men like Elston Howard do not seem to be handicapped by that, so it is probably just a matter of which glove you are more comfortable with.

To keep your bare fingers out of the way, you do not clench them but just hold the bare hand lightly closed, so the fingers will be folded out of the way. A foul tip on a tightly clenched finger can break it too. Many catchers, like Howard, take hold of the outer rim of the glove with the bare hand, and thus remind themselves to keep that hand folded until the ball is safely in the glove.

The basic position for the catcher to take while awaiting the pitch is a solid, well-spread stance, with knees flexed and the flat part of the glove held up like a target right in front of the catcher's chest. While it is important to be able to move out of that position with the quickness of a cat, you should not shift or wobble or move around while awaiting the pitch. Give the pitcher a good solid target and hold it until the pitch is on its way.

When you receive the ball, you should let both hands "give" with the pitch so that they ride right up toward the throwing position. (This is not possible, of course, when you have to scramble or scrape for the pitch.) The habit of going automatically into throwing position is a good one for a catcher to develop. Split seconds make the difference between safe or out on a steal. So you catch the ball in the glove, cover it instantly with the meat hand, then let them ride together to the right and up. Get the ball into your throwing hand quickly and be ready to let it fly.

Before I start talking about throwing to bases, I want to complete what I have to say about catching or stopping the ball. Don't take chances on letting pitches get by you. Don't stay anchored on your position on a wide pitch and try to Fancy Dan it by reaching your arm across your body. Hop or slide right over to get your body in the way of the pitch, then glove it in your regular fashion if you can. If you can't, you'll at least have your body in the way so the ball is less likely to go sailing off toward the seats behind you.

On a pitch that hits the dirt in front of you—and you will get plenty of those, and even call for them occasionally—you do not try to field the ball the way a baseman would. That is, you don't fret too much about making a clean pickup. Your first thought is to close up all the avenues through which the ball might skip by. So you drop right to your knees in front of the pitch and use your glove to close the space left open between your thighs. This way, you will at least keep the ball in front of you. And unless the baserunner has taken off before the pitch, you still have a chance to pick up the ball and flag him down.

If you ever look at old-time pictures of baseball games, you may notice that the catcher was often a good long stride behind the plate. Nowadays, catchers believe in staying close—just as close to the batter as they can stand, without danger of interfering with the bat. This not only gives the catcher a better chance to get out after a bunt, it also helps him in fielding foul flies, for it gives him a quicker start and more room to work.

It helps his pitcher too because the catcher will be catching low pitches in the strike zone and making it easier for the umpire to call them properly.

While your stance in general is a half crouch, there are many times when you may want to squat low, or even go to one knee, so as to provide a solid low target for a pitcher who is having trouble getting his pitches down. The signals to the pitcher are always given in a full crouch, of course. You squat right down on your heels and lay your fingers on the inside of your right thigh. You hold your glove out on your left knee to shut off the view of the third-base coach. Once the sign has been seen and accepted, you get into your catching stance. You will probably have one foot a little ahead of the other, with the feet well spread, because this gives you a firmer footing and enables you to spring in any direction after a ball or to make a throw.

Most catchers today like to keep one finger outside the glove to provide extra protection for the first joint, which takes most of the impact. A lot of pounding on that joint can slow the circulation, numb your finger a bit, and make it harder to glove the pitches deftly.

In making your throws to the base, you have to be full of confidence. The catcher who hesitates to throw is the man the baserunners will take liberties with. They will hold the big lead after the pitch, or they will be moving toward the next base instead of skipping back where they started. When you see a baserunner getting too free with his lead, and failing to return to his spot near the base after the pitch, let fly. Step right out toward the base and let the ball go without windup, from right behind your head. If you throw to second, you throw right straight at the base, so the ball will get there about knee-high. And you step right out over the plate toward second base as you throw. Put all your muscle into the throw. Don't be halfhearted about it or try to steer the ball by letting it go at half speed. You have to keep practicing a full-strength throw, even if the first fifty you try go right to the outfield fence. Practice and more practice will bring these throws closer and closer to the target, until finally you will *know* you can hit the target any time you want. Wild throws in practice should never dishearten you. I would rather see a young catcher heave a dozen balls into center field than see him choke up on his throws and try to flip the ball down as if he were pitching horseshoes.

A fast throw to first base will help keep a runner close and will also remind him that he cannot get funny with you. Often you can get a runner half asleep there if you step toward first base quickly, after taking the pitch, and fire the ball down full strength. Only make sure there is somebody there to take the throw. Ideally, the throw should go down inside the baseline, as on any tag play. You must also make sure a runner on third does not hold too long a lead. If you catch him dawdling part way down the baseline after a pitch, bang the ball down. Step right out of your position toward third and let the ball fly. The knowledge that you can and will let a throw go down will make your bluff throws far more effective and will keep the runner from getting off to a big start on a ground ball.

All the great catchers I ever saw, up to and including our own Andy Etchebarren, have been quick to move out of their position and get off a throw to any base. That is one of the major contributions a catcher can make—to keep baserunners close and to cut them down when they get too fancy.

But the fielding play a catcher makes most frequently, outside of receiving the pitches, is catching pop fouls. This ought to be an easy play, and for most catchers it is. But if you try to make it too easy, if you are offhand about it and fail to concentrate on the catch with your full mind, then you can look awfully foolish. Once the ball has been fouled off, your first job is to *find* it. Turn quickly, get your mask off with an upward sweep of your meat hand, and locate the ball. When you *know* where it is and know you have at least an outside chance of getting to it, toss the mask *away* from where the ball is coming down and scramble to get under the ball. If you have time—and you usually do—position yourself under the ball so it seems to be coming right down on your nose. Then get your glove high, palm up, and take it in *both* hands at about eye level. If you get your glove high, you often will have a second chance at the catch if you should miss it the first time.

Frequently, if you are playing in a park with a double- or triple-deck grandstand, the balls that seem to be coming down into the stand, or onto the screen, will spin away from the stands as they come down, so it is a good idea not to give up on these too soon.

On infield pop flies, or foul pops up the baselines that you have a chance for, you let the pitcher captain the play. Ordinarily, the man with the baseman's glove can handle a pop fly better than you can, so do not insist on trying for one when you are called off. But don't give up on *any* ball until someone else yells for it.

The catcher must also be on his toes to field a bunt, for he is often the closest player to the ball and in the best position to make a throw to a base. In almost every instance, you should follow a bunt to the left as this will keep your body in position to get off a throw to first base without an awkward twisting or shifting around. When a bunt goes right up the third-base line, and stays fair, you will probably find it quicker to trail the ball to the right then turn completely to get off your throw to the base. A bunt should always be fielded in both hands and you should keep your eye right on the ball until you have hold of it. Many a putout is missed because the man fielding the bunt tries to make too offhand a play out of it, trying to pluck the ball off the ground while he is watching the runner or watching first base. Sometimes you can do this. More often you will miss the ball completely and will still be grabbing at it when the runner speeds across the base.

Use your glove to round the ball up and your bare hand to take hold of it. But bend right down and get close to the ball and never take your eye from it until you have it tight in your throwing hand. Then fire the ball down *inside* the baseline, hard and fast. Sometimes, you will pick up a sacrifice bunt quickly enough to have a chance to put out the lead runner. Of course you will have considered the possibility *before* the bunt was made, so you won't be startled to find a runner going down to second, or down to third. The pitcher or another player will probably be shouting to you to throw to second, or to third, if you have a chance. But do not throw blindly, just because someone told you where to throw. Take a look and use your own judgment as to whether you will beat the runner. And be sure too that there is a fielder there to take your throw. You cannot afford to bluff a throw or to think the situation over. You have got to make up your mind instantly, or you may lose the man going down to first.

Baseline bunts that have a chance of going foul should be allowed to roll. Once the ball trickles into foul territory, brush it right away with your glove, so it will be instantly out of play. Don't ever wait for it to roll fair again. If there is doubt in your mind as to whether a ball is fair or foul—whether it has bounced on the plate, for instance—play it safe and make the putout. Don't anticipate the umpire's decision.

But now let's get back to your main job, helping the pitcher get the batters out. The catcher, being closer to the batter and being (supposedly) more knowledgeable anyway about hitters and their habits, is usually given the job of calling the pitches. But in practice you and your pitcher decide between you how to deal with the opposing batters. If you know a pitcher well and know that his good pitches are working, you will probably disagree very seldom on what to throw at any time. If the pitcher does disagree with you, however, you have to let him have his way, for you never want a pitcher to throw a pitch that he does not want to throw. If there is some reason for throwing the pitch you called for, something you can see and the pitcher cannot—perhaps some weakness you have detected in the batter—then ask for time and go explain matters to your pitcher. Make sure he is convinced.

Sometimes a pitcher will want to get fancy when there is no need— out of fear that a good hitter may tee off on his fast ball, perhaps. Then you have to go out and emphasize to the pitcher the need to go with his best pitch in a clutch. Or he may be reluctant to "pitch around" a heavy hitter. Again you have to convince him that there is no need to take chances. But the pitcher has to go along with you, or you must give him his way.

A catcher has to be a part-time psychologist in dealing with pitchers. Some are too easy to convince. Some are too headstrong. The Yanks had a pitcher once who would throw fancy pitches regardless of what you threatened him with. He always had something new he wanted to try and the trouble was that when he was right he was just about unhittable, so he had good basis for his faith in his own judgment. Then there are other pitchers who need encouragement all the time, who have a tendency to get down on themselves whenever anyone gets a hit. These are the fellows who need a lot of building up, a lot of patting on the back, a lot of reminding that the hit was pure luck. As a matter of fact, every pitcher has to be encouraged all the time. Flattery will go a long way with all the pitchers I ever met. You have to tell them how good their pitches are and how great a job they have been doing. Sometimes, when three batters in a row have put the good pitch out in the deep grass, this takes some doing; but you have to keep talking it up.

A few pitchers need to be needled into giving the job their very best. These are the guys who, after a few strong innings, will begin to coast. Maybe they think they are getting tired. Maybe they don't feel the pressure that makes them put out their best. So then you must supply the pressure. Make them get their backs into the pitch. If they have a good lead, urge them to throw nothing but strikes, to make the enemy work to get on.

Of course if a pitcher really is tired, then you have to be ready to let the manager know. If the pitcher begins to throw "straight up"—that is, without bending right into the pitch—you can suspect that he is wearing out. Also you must watch him to make sure his motion is natural, and that he is not favoring a sore spot, or trying to conceal a weakness.

In dealing with the hitters, your general aim is to make the man hit the pitch you want him to—the "out" pitch that will turn into a simple chance in the infield or outfield. And so you undertake to set him up for this pitch, by pulling him up close to the plate or pushing him away, by showing him a bad high pitch to get him ready for a low one. But you do not let this aim persuade you to start off by showing him weak pitches. It used to be that most batters would take the first pitch—that is, let it go in order to size the pitcher up. But nowadays a great many hitters will land on the first pitch if it is anywhere near what they want. So, still speaking generally, we advise a pitcher to make the first pitch a good one, a strike with something on it, so that he has a chance of getting ahead of the hitter.

When you are working with one of the fireball pitchers—those rare fellows of the caliber of Turley, Lonborg, Score, Feller, and McDowell —you know you are going to get a bagful of strikeouts. These fellows will upset a hitter's timing just by the incredible speed with which their pitches explode toward the plate, so there is seldom a need to get too fancy in "setting up" a hitter. But even they can help themselves often by showing another pitch, so the batter cannot set himself too solidly. Even if they cannot use the curve effectively, you can call for it to be thrown out of the strike zone now and then, and it will help keep the batter honest. If one of these fellows can control his curve and his slider, then he is murder. He will also probably have a long career. But just the same you have to remember that his best pitch is the fast ball and that is what you should depend on when the situation is tight. As a matter of fact, a good fast ball has no real peer as a pitch to get hitters out with.

A hitter of course is thinking right along with you and the pitcher. He is up there to make you give him the pitch he wants and he will try to hang on until he gets it, or something like it. If you know what he likes to hit—and in the big leagues, you should—you can take care not to offer it to him, or if you do offer it, ask for it out of the strike zone, where he probably cannot do any damage with it.

Sometimes catchers forget that the club should be playing together to get the batter out. If, for instance, there is a man on base, the hitter may by trying to hit behind him—to put the ball into right field to move the batter along. The fielders will be positioning themselves in expectation of that. And you can help by calling for a tight pitch against a right-handed batter—one that he will have a hard time putting into right field, that he may even pop up if he tries to place it there. With a left-handed batter, you will offer him outside pitches. And you will check your fielders to see that they are ready to field the blow that might result. If your shortstop is far over toward second base, an outside pitch to a left-hander may be just what the batter needs to put through the hole at shortstop. You may have to hold up proceedings while you get the fielders straightened out on what you are trying to accomplish.

We always teach our batters to study the catcher rather than the pitcher, on the ground that it is the catcher who sets the pitching pattern, and the catcher's habits rather than the pitcher's that show up from game to game. It is good practice then to check yourself and make sure you are not getting into a static pattern of high-and-tight, low-and-away, or some such arrangement, that the hitters can prepare for. You and the pitcher have to try always to keep the hitter off balance and keep him from getting what he is looking for.

But bear in mind always that good hitters can learn to hit almost any sort of pitch. A man who dotes on fast balls may get so many curves that he learns to do even better with them, and his weakness may turn into a strength. This has happened many times in the big leagues. Mickey Mantle for instance always wanted fast balls. But before he had been around more than a few years he could put a slow curve into the stands too and often did so.

When you are trying to deal with hitters you have not seen before, as most catchers do in amateur and school ball, you can learn a lot about them by watching them take their practice cuts and by observing the way they stand at the plate. The Nervous Nellies who keep shifting the hind foot, afraid to dig in, are the ones who will flinch from a crossfire, or a good tight pitch. The man who stands far from the plate can be set up with an inside pitch, out of the strike zone, and made to fish after the low outside curve. The fellow who likes to edge up on the plate when he has two strikes on him can sometimes be finished off with a good hard pitch on the inside. The hungry hitters, the cowtailers who swing the full length of a heavy bat and are impatient to lay the wood on the ball, can sometimes be struck out on a pitch that goes right into the dirt. And you must not be afraid to call for such a pitch (by pointing to the ground) when you have one of these fellows up there straining at the leash.

With a runner on base, the catcher's job becomes doubly complicated. If there is a man on first, it is up to the catcher to keep the pitcher alive to the fact that there is a runner there. If you think the runner is taking too much lead on the pitcher, point to first base and tell the pitcher plainly to hold that runner close. And of course you check to make sure after every pitch that the runner is not holding onto his lead.

Sometimes you can arrange a pickoff play at first, especially when the first baseman is moving in for a bunt. Then the second baseman, on a signal from you, can dash for the bag to take a quick throw, which should come to him of course on the second base side of the bag where he can get it right on a sliding runner without wasted motion.

When there is a runner on second base, you can make a practice of trying for him any time he holds onto his lead after the pitch, and allows the shortstop to get closer to the base than he is. Or you can work out a sign with pitcher and shortstop, so that you can indicate whenever the shortstop is closer to the base than the runner. Then, on an agreed count, the pitcher, without any previous look, can turn and fire the ball to the base.

The man on third is always the major danger, of course, and you should not allow him any liberties. Besides making sure he does not stray too far, and gets back to the base after the pitch, you can work out a play to trap him on a double steal, when a man tries for second while the man on third tries for home. The shortstop can sometimes cut in behind the pitching mound, and take a good hard throw from you that looks as if it were meant for second base, then fire it right back in time to catch the lead runner. You can also trap a runner off third sometimes with a good bluff throw to second. But it must be a good piece of acting on your part, not just a sort of feint. You will have to step right out over the plate and fire hard with your throwing arm—but hang tight to the ball. Then turn and bang the ball down for real to third base, inside the baseline. Only you must be sure you have a fielder there to take your throw.

When the bases are empty, the catcher becomes a part-time infielder, running down to back up first base any time there will be a play there. This is an important task and can pay big dividends. Nine times out of ten, you'll have no work to do, because not many throws get by the first baseman in organized baseball. But that tenth time can be the time you keep a runner from advancing to put an important run on second base. In backing up the base, you must take care not to get too close, or a bad throw will skip right through the first baseman and you as well. The proper distance is about a third of the baseline distance—twenty-five or thirty feet.

The one play that seems to cause most nervousness among prospective catchers is putting the tag on a runner at home. But this is not nearly so bad a job as it might seem, and very few catchers have ever been hurt at it. You must simply remember that you have no right to block the plate if you do not hold the ball. Then, if you have got the ball, keep it in both hands—that is, wrapped tight in your meat hand and protected by your glove—when you attempt to put the tag on the runner. You do not of course have to leave the whole plate clear as you await the throw. But you must offer the runner an open crack at the plate until you have the ball in your hands. A throw that is coming in from the outfield will ordinarily bounce in front of the plate. You wait for such a throw right behind the plate and step forward up the baseline to meet the runner when you get the ball. Shorter throws may be taken in front of the plate; then you can close off the plate with one foot and put the tag on the runner as he slides in. There is no need to engage in a contest with him to see who can knock the other over. Just put the tag on him and get out of there. Naturally if the throw is off target, you will have to abandon the plate and go get the ball. Often, however, you can put the tag on with a last-minute lunge. Just do not attempt to throw yourself across the base-line. Go for the runner with the ball held in both hands. What he does after you have put the tag on him does not matter, as long as he does not run over you. Some catchers, even holding the ball, will always leave a slice of the plate for the runner to aim at, and count on tagging him as he goes by. That is far safer than trying to plop down in front of the plate where the man must crash into you, or dive over you.

There are many plays in which the throw to the plate must be cut off in the infield so that the run is conceded and an effort is made to catch a runner at another base. The catcher is the man who must decide, in something less than the blink of an eye, whether he has a chance to make a putout at the plate. If he sees that the throw is going to be too late then he must yell "Cut it off!" so the cutoff man can intercept the throw and make the other play. But if he sees he has a chance to cut off the run, he will shout "Let it go!" and make ready to receive the throw himself.

Do not forget that baserunners are allowed to advance after a foul fly has been caught (if the catch does not make the third out). When there is a runner on base and you have to go a long way back to catch a foul, turn and be ready to throw the ball. If you are far behind the plate, you will need to throw to the pitcher, who will have come down toward the plate to act as relay man. Just don't go to sleep on this play, because the runner can start as soon as the ball touches your glove.

A catcher usually sets the tone for a ball club's play. If he is aggressive and alert, he can keep the whole club on its toes, and he can keep the pitcher working hard. There are ballplayers who tend to let down when they have a big lead on the opposition. It is not that they loaf or deliberately goof off. They just do not feel the pressure of tight competition and so do not call up that last little bit of effort that so often makes the difference between a win and a loss. A catcher can go a long way toward keeping such a player right in the ball game, by talking it up, by aggressive play of his own, getting that ball around the infield with plenty of zip after an out, holding runners tight, celebrating the strikeouts, encouraging the pitcher. A catcher must keep his cool too, when things go wrong. It is up to him to help the pitcher steady down, to hold onto the ball a little longer when the pitcher is working too fast, to encourage the infielder who boots a ball, and to keep the first baseman and third baseman alive to the possibilities of a bunt.

And he must, as I said, work with the rest of the club in trying to get the opposition out. With a man on first, and less than two out, he must call for those low pitches that will produce the double-play ball. If he has a notorious hit-and-run man up, he must try to keep him from hitting to right. When a bunt is in order, however, he does not usually try too hard to keep the batter from bunting, unless a squeeze play is impending. He does not, that is, take chances on walking a man just to keep him from sacrificing. There is no percentage in that at all. But if there are runs on base and a big hitter up, he does help the pitcher to "pitch around" him, to give him nothing good in the strike zone, as long as first base is open. Often it is better to walk such a man than have him break up the ball game, and the pitcher's morale, with a long blow. And sometimes such a hitter will be impatient enough to go after one of those bad pitches and pop out.

If you have a potential run on third, with less than two out and the score tight, your infield may be drawn in to keep that run from crossing the plate. In a situation like that you must avoid calling for the high pitches, the ones that can be looped out over the heads of the drawn-in infielders.

You may have to remind the fielders too to help the pitcher by adjusting to the batter and the situation, to come in for the short line drives with the winning run on third in the last of the ninth and less than two out, for instance. In that situation a long drive is bound to score a run even if it is caught, so the only thing you must guard against is the shorter blow that might land in front of a fielder if he is playing too far out.

Above all, do not get anchored in your own position, for you will have the baseball in your hands as often as anyone outside the pitcher and it is up to you to be ready to move when you can make a throw or a play that will help your pitcher. To this end, you should take care not to settle down into a deep squat with men on base. Let everyone see you are ready to move out and throw at any time, and be ready for whatever might develop. Take care not to crouch with your elbows inside your knees, at any time, for you can get yourself locked into a position like that and be unable to move out fast after a bunt or a pop foul.

Each pitcher will present you with different problems, and you must know just what to expect. The fireball man may have a tendency to work too fast, to let the hitters set the pace of the proceeding. Then you will have to hang onto the ball after each pitch, even walk part way out before returning it. Or he may, like so many of those bullet throwers, have a tendency to go wild high. Then you will have to take care to give him a good low target, even getting the glove right on the ground at times to make sure that low curve comes down and does not hang up there where the hitter can lace it out to the fence. Or he may make the mistake some young pitchers make, of easing up on the tail end of the batting order, and using off-speed stuff against the weak hitters. You will have to remind him that these weak hitters must provide him his outs and should be overpowered. Off-speed stuff may be all they can hit consistently.

You will occasionally find that your pitcher is off the target with his good pitch. Then you will have to ask for that as his waste pitch and depend instead on the second best. As the innings go by, you will very likely find that he has begun to get his good pitch into the strike zone consistently again. Then you can switch tactics and use one of his other pitches as the waste pitch.

In short you will have to be using your brain as well as your eyes and muscles all the while, to adjust to changing situations, to help make your pitcher effective, to keep runners close, and to field everything in your reach. And all the while, concentrate on your major job—to keep that ball from getting by.

1. Andy Etchebarren prefers this old-fashioned type of catcher's glove, with no break in the rim. The new trapper-type, he says, makes him a one-handed catcher.

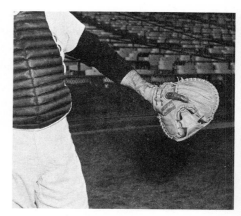

2. Like most catchers, Andy keeps one finger outside the glove as he works, to ease the pounding on the joint. Notice that Andy is wearing an inner glove too. He also has a piece of sponge rubber inside the glove.

3. Andy catches the ball on one knee, if there are no runners on base. This enables him to give the pitcher the sort of low target all pitchers prefer.

4. With a runner on base, Andy goes into a crouch like this. He still gives a good low target, but he is ready to jump right out and throw the ball at any time. He keeps his elbows outside his knees so as not to get locked into position.

5. This is Andy signaling for number one—the fast ball. He lays his finger against his thigh and holds his glove out at his knee to keep the enemy coach from stealing the sign.

6. When Andy throws to second, he steps right out toward the base and lets fly from behind his ear. His toe is pointed straight at second and he throws right at the base, trying to get the ball there about knee-high.

7. On a foul pop, Andy's first job is to get that mask off, which he does with a quick upward sweep of his right hand.

8. Then he locates the ball. He hangs onto the mask until he knows exactly where the ball is.

9. Andy throws the mask away from the ball and tries to get directly under the ball, so it seems to be coming right down on his head.

10. Andy catches the ball high, so that if it gets away from him he may have another grab at it.

11. In fielding a bunt, Andy gets rid of the mask in a hurry and scrambles right out, to the *left* of the ball.

12. He fields the bunt with both hands, with his head down and his back and knees bent.

◎

THE PITCHER

It is pretty obvious I guess that I like a big pitching staff. I don't mean big pitchers, because good ones come almost any size, but a great plenty of strong pitchers, so that I never have to work a man past his capacity or leave a man in when he is getting bombed, and can hit for my pitchers if need be, without putting a strain on my bullpen. For starters I like strong young fellows with lots of competitive spirit, men who really enjoy challenging the hitters and men who can throw a fast ball that shows some life. For relief pitchers I like the experienced hands with lots of cuteness, or fireballers who can really explode that ball in there full strength for three or four innings.

To be effective as a starter a pitcher has got to have more than one pitch. Dave McNally, who by my standards has the best curve ball in the league, would not be nearly so good with it if he did not also have a live fast ball, one that moves as it comes to the plate. And Wally Bunker's good fast ball would be a lot less effective if he did not have that amazing sinker to go along with it.

Still, when a pitcher starts out in life he is best advised to begin with his fast ball and to work to control it. A fast ball comes from strong arms and back and strong legs. And these are developed through lots of hard work—throwing and running. A throwing arm will last a long time if it is properly developed and properly used. I don't mean that it should be babied. Quite the opposite. It should be used full strength. But it should *always* be warmed up, in warm weather or cool, and it should not be worked when it is hurt. Stiffness and ache

that come from using it properly do not mean it is hurt. They can
be worked out by careful warming up and steady work. But bruises
and tears and twists have to be fully healed before you put strain
on your arm. And any injury that causes you to alter your stride or
your motion should be all cured before you undertake to pitch steadily.

When you throw, whether to warm up or while playing ball in
any form, you should take care to throw at a target. This is the way
you train your eyes and muscles to coordinate. Random throwing does
not help your control nor develop your arm properly. Even if you
throw rocks for fun, pick out something to aim at. Take care too
always to take a step when you throw, so you do not develop an
unnatural motion that will strain your back.

When you begin to pitch, the best target to aim at is a low one.
Aim at the knee or the belt buckle of the man who is catching your
pitches, or try to hit him in mid-thigh. Keep your eye on the target
as you throw. But do not steer your pitches. That is, do not use
half-strength throws or pushes, to hit the target dead-center. Reach
back the full length of your arm, getting your elbow free of your body,
and throw (when you are warmed up) with all your strength. Do
not be too concerned if you keep missing the target, even if you miss
by several feet. Your job is to learn to control a full-strength pitch.
Just flipping the ball carefully to the right spot is of no value to you.
You might do that a hundred times and still miss the target by a
bat length when you start to throw hard.

During this part of your training, forget about trick pitches. You'll
need extra pitches eventually, but none of them will be any use to you
until you can control your fast ball, and practicing trick pitches can
delay the proper development of your arm. Just stick to the job of
learning to throw a fast ball *low*. Remember the high pitches are the
extra-base pitches. The low pitches produce the ground balls and the
double plays. Don't bother with a plate to begin with. Just use the
catcher's body for a target and concentrate on keeping the ball below
the waist. After you have developed this "up-and-down" control you
will be ready to practice keeping the ball over the plate. You will
find this is relatively simple, once you have learned to keep the ball
down.

The time to start practicing your curve ball is after you have got
control of your fast ball. As a matter of fact you can probably pitch

some winning baseball long before you have perfected control of your curve. I have an idea that a lot of young fellows fail to develop as pitchers because they think of pitching mainly as the throwing of dipsy-doodle pitches and they put in most of their time trying to fool batters with that sort of stuff. So they never put in the hours and hours of full-strength throwing that it takes to make an arm strong and keep it that way. Perhaps if they just stuck to trying to knock tin cans off fences with rocks they would do a lot better. But assuming you have got your fast ball under control and understand that it will probably always be your best pitch, you can start on your curve. It is not a hard pitch to throw and is not going to hurt your arm. As a matter of fact, in some ways it is an easier pitch than the fast ball. A straight overhand fast ball is hard on the shoulder in some ways because I don't believe the shoulder is made to bring the arm around like a windmill. A three-quarter motion, between sidearm and overhand, is far more natural. And it is a motion that can also produce a very good curve, so that you will be using exactly the same motion for both pitches.

When you throw your fast ball, you hold the ball between the tips of the first two fingers and the tip of the thumb and you let it fly straight off those points as you bring your arm down. Some pitchers fuss about whether they have the seams rotating all four toward the batter, but I was never convinced that that made so much difference. If you have a good tight hold on the ball, it is going to spin and act alive when you throw it straight.

The curve ball is held a little deeper in the hand than the fast ball (some pitchers give their curve away by looking down to see if they have the ball properly adjusted in their hands) and it is released, not off the tips of the fingers but off the edge of the index finger, out of the crotch between thumb and index finger. This means that the hand must be rotated at the wrist as it comes down in the pitching motion, and when the ball is released, the palm is upward. If you try this in slow motion, you will probably discover that it is easier to throw a curve sidearm, or that it is more natural to do it that way. But unless you can throw a good fast ball sidearm, don't try it this way. A sidearm curve curves away from the batter, but it does not sink, while an overhand curve spins both *down* and away, making it much harder to meet with the bat. A good sidearm crossfire, which seems to approach the batter from the vicinity of third or first base (depending on whether the pitcher is right- or left-handed) is a very effective weapon at times and some fast ball pitchers will go in for that occasionally. But you should be able to throw your curve off the fast ball motion if you really want to keep the hitter off balance.

I have not said anything about windup, because that is really a matter of personal preference. There are some pitchers who find they have better control without any windup at all, so they use the same motion at all times, with bases empty or occupied. But ordinarily a pitcher goes into some sort of rocking or pumping motion to get all his muscles working together—just as a coxswain gives a "count" to keep all oars pulling in the same rhythm, and a football kicker takes a step and a half to build up momentum. I suppose in the old days, pitchers wound up like windmills so they could let the ball fly with centrifugal force, built up in five or six rapid revolutions. But that sort of pitching went out with high shoes. Now you have all sorts of different windups, all supposed to help a pitcher gather up all his strength for the pitch—or to give the appearance that he is going to throw full strength.

No matter how you wind up, your best method of delivery will be basically the same as every pitcher uses. You will start with a backward motion, to get your arm fully extended behind you. To do this properly, you must move your forward foot (right foot for a right-hander) from its position with the toe on the rubber, and plant it parallel to the rubber, in the hole you make right in front of the rubber. Your shoe must keep contact with the rubber as you do this. Then you swing your other leg up to maintain your balance properly as you reach back. Your knees as you do this are slightly bent. You stride forward with this uplifted leg as you pitch, and ideally you land on your toe and bring your right foot (left if a left-hander) up alongside the other one as you follow through, so you land knees bent, feet parallel, facing the batter and ready to field a ball.

Fireball pitchers often take an extra long stride. And additional power is provided by a good *shove* off the rubber by the foot that has remained in contact with it. An extra long stride usually means that you cannot come down on the toe of the front foot as you should, so you compensate for that by landing with bent knee. (There are a few good fast ball pitchers who land flat-footed and stiff-kneed.

Jim Bunning does. But he also topples off the mound frequently on his follow-through and winds up on all fours. Hitters just don't hit him often enough for it to matter.)

When you throw your curve, you should shorten your stride a little, to give you more room in which to apply the spinning motion to the ball. If you can think of the ball as being attached to a string that is wound around inside it as it might be inside a spinning toy and the string as being attached to some imaginary point above your head, you can understand that the longer "pull" you make, the more spin you will get on the ball. So you shorten your stride to give a longer "pull." On a short stride, you will notice that the distance between the top of your reach and the point of release is a longer arc. But again you should come down on your toe, with knees bent.

Of course the curve will be effective only if you learn how to keep it in the strike zone. This is something you learn through practice, just as you learned to control the fast ball. You have to keep throwing the curve full strength at targets until you develop the proper coordination between eye and muscle to enable you to put that curve where you want it to go. But if your fast ball is effective you can work on your curve during a ball game, using it as a waste pitch—one that you know will not come into the strike zone—merely to help upset the batter's timing.

With the fast ball working and the curve ball coming along, you can think about the change-of-pace pitch—which may be all you need to make you a complete pitcher. The curve is in a sense a change-of-pace, because it approaches the plate with somewhat less speed than the fast ball. And some pitchers use a change-of-pace off the curve ball motion, because it is probably easier to throw that way. I think, however, that the best change-of-pace is the one that is thrown off the fast ball motion. It is a lot more deceptive, just because it is apparently thrown with all the power you own, and will look just like the fast ball as it starts toward the plate.

There are all sorts of "changes." There is the "slip" pitch that Steve Barber uses. There is the fork ball that Warren Spahn was so effective with. There are knuckle balls and fingertip balls and the various "illegal" pitches, such as the spitter and the "Vaseline ball." They all have the same general purpose: to diminish the friction caused by the grip of the fingers on the ball. That is why a change-up used to be called a "thumb ball"—because the thumb provided the only spin, counteracting the fingers and causing the ball to ride up to the plate with so little spin that you could see the stitches. This also, of course, greatly diminished the speed.

Perhaps the easiest change-up to throw is the one that is held fast ball style, except that the ball is gripped on top not by the fingertips, but by the middle joints of the fingers, and on the bottom by the first joint of the thumb. You go through the same arm motion as with a fast ball, but you lift your fingertips *off* the ball just as you release it. You also have to be careful not to get too much body shove into this ball. You want all the motion with little of the effect. When you practice this pitch, keep your hind foot (your pivot foot) out of it. Instead of bringing it up quickly to land parallel to your front foot, leave it on the rubber until you have completed your entire motion. That will prevent you from getting too much "oomph" into the pitch.

You will have to work on this baby a long time before you learn to control it, but it will be time well invested. You are going to see a lot of these change-ups go flying into the yonder, or bouncing on the ground before you begin to get them into the strike zone. But keep working until you discover just how to throw the pitch to bring it into the right spots. When you have it well under control, you can begin to practice taking your hind foot off the rubber and just dragging it up to its place alongside the other foot, without any shove or bounce. Then you will have a good, effective change-up that will greatly increase your effectiveness, and you will have the fun of seeing some good strong batters misjudge the pitch completely and stride out so far ahead of time that they are unable to get legs and back into the swing and can just flap at the ball weakly with the bat. That is a sight a pitcher can really grow fat on.

The other pitches—the slider, the sinker, the screwball—that are popular today are not really necessary to an effective career, but they can help keep you on top; learning to throw one of them will make you that much more of a pitcher, as long as it does not interfere with your control of your basic weapons—fast ball and curve. Probably the most effective pitch, or the one that most pitchers find effective, is the slider. I have an idea that the slider is one of the major reasons why batting averages in late years have stayed so low. It is a long long time since anyone got close enough under .400 to tickle it.

The slider is called all sorts of pet names: Fast ball curve, nickel curve, and whatnot. It is a ball that curves very slightly away from a batter—away from a right-handed batter when a right-handed pitcher throws it. Yet it is thrown like a fast ball with fast ball motion and approaches the plate with the speed of a fast ball. The spin that makes it curve away is supplied by a sort of cutting motion at the completion of the pitch, as if you had decided at the last second to make this into a curve. The index finger supplies almost no pressure on this pitch. It is all done by the middle one. Because the ball is held in the fingertips, not as deep as a curve, it does not get the full spin—just enough to move it out of the straight line it might have followed. What you do really is give it about half the curve ball wrist rotation, then let it fly. This critter needs a lot of practice too and it should get your attention only when you have everything else well under control. It is effective only when combined with a good fast ball and curve.

The sinker is another pitch that drives some batters to drink. It is especially effective against the guys who like to rattle the high pitches off the fence, for it keeps them hitting over the ball and bouncing it into the infield. This is thrown screwball style, with the wrist turning the "wrong" way, away from the batter instead of toward him. As a result the ball breaks down and in, mostly down. It differs from the screwball, or reverse curve, only in that it lacks the sharp wrist rotation that gives reverse spin. The sinker cannot be thrown with full body effort, and so on this pitch you also must practice leaving your hind foot on the rubber as you throw, or just dragging it slowly off the rubber, without any shove.

Knuckle balls and fingernail or fingertip balls move without any spin because they are not thrown so much as they are pushed, with the hand held behind the ball rather than over it. You use the same motion as you would on your fast ball, except that you keep your wrist stiff. That is, you do not cock the wrist as you ordinarily do in any straight throw. This takes a good deal of doing and it is not a ball for young pitchers to grow up on, unless you just fiddle with it as you develop your arm by regular fast ball and curve.

The knuckle ball is not popular with catchers because its flight is too erratic. Its sudden appearance, out of the fast ball motion, makes it seem to stand still for a split second and "flutter." Then it will dip out of the straight course before it reaches the plate and may go in almost any direction, so a catcher has to snatch at it at the last second. Those big gloves may be useful in stopping the ball, even after you have misjudged its target by several inches. But they are mighty hard to catch with. I think a catcher with quick hands, who is willing to hold off to the last instant and then just grab for the pitch, will handle the knuckler with fewer passed balls.

Operating with men on base requires a different stance and different concentration. There are certain things the pitcher is not permitted to do when he is on the mound. He is not permitted to fake a throw toward first base, and he is not permitted to take a stance on or near the mound or make pitching motions when he is not in possession of the ball. If he does move toward first with foot or arm while on the rubber, he is required to complete his throw there. Because a windup would give the runner a long head start, the pitcher stands with his pivot foot parallel to the rubber and in contact with it, and his other foot a short stride ahead. That is, a right-hander in the stretch position has his left foot advanced. He still takes a stride forward with that foot and shoves off with the other foot, and of course he reaches back before he pitches. A well-schooled pitcher, however, can develop a motion that will look just the same in all its preliminaries, no matter whether he is going to throw to first or throw home. That is, he will lift the front leg, raise the ball in both hands, reach out behind him with the ball—and still be able to stride toward first as well as toward home.

But you should not, if you are pitching with men on base, allow the runner to upset your concentration. If you are going to throw to first, you must decide to do that as you start your motion and not let it be a sudden impulse. Keep watch on the man's feet. You can do that without turning your head right at him. If he is too far off first, or seems to be moving toward second, pump and stride toward first and throw there so the ball will reach the baseman on the second-base side of the bag. Do this as often as you must, until you have succeeded in getting the runner back closer to the bag or in having him lean back toward first. Of course, if the man has a really daring lead or persists in walking toward second base, you may have to snap the ball over without any fake pitching motion. Sometimes you can stop one of these walkers by just lifting your hind foot off the rubber and placing it behind the rubber, thus freeing you from the "balk" restrictions (except that you must have hold of the ball). Sometimes all you need to do is turn your head and look at the man, actually stare him down until he stops and moves back. If he still keeps going, then back off the rubber and move right toward him, with the ball in your hand. He'll go back then, or else find himself hung up on the baseline.

Once you have got the man back as close to the bag as you want him to be, or with his weight leaning back toward first, so he cannot get a good start, then you can go to the plate with your pitch. Before you do that, put the runner right out of your mind and concentrate entirely on the batter.

The runner on second is easier for you to deal with, because you are allowed to make feints toward him without penalty. And sometimes if you have a slow man on the bag who is foolish enough to take a big lead, you may let him keep it so the catcher can nail him right after the pitch. Or you may have a pickoff play worked out with the catcher, who will indicate that one of your fielders is closer to the bag than the runner is. This is a "count" play, in which you do not even turn toward the base until you have counted to a certain number in a rhythm you have practiced. Then you turn and fire the ball to the base and you know that the fielder will be there to take the throw.

The man on third can distract you if you let him. One thing you must never do about him is forget him. If he is allowed to wander too far down the baseline, he can steal home on a pitch. So you watch him as you take your position on the rubber and keep your eye on him as you stretch. If he keeps moving toward the plate, of course you have got to play for him. But usually if you keep watching him, he will get back closer to the bag and look to see where the baseman is. Once you have him where he belongs, or moving in that direction, you can put him out of your mind and pitch to the plate.

There are many refinements you will learn as you practice pitching with men on base—pickoff plays with the first baseman, "change-of-pace" throws to first, and other combinations designed to prevent steals, bluff runners into trying to advance, or killing off the lead runner on a sacrifice. These are the sort of things you learn only by playing the game. The "change-of-pace" to first base, for instance, usually works only with a slow-witted or absentminded runner, or an inexperienced one. It consists simply of throwing to first at moderate speed two or three times and then following with a really sizzling throw. Sometimes you will get a runner into a certain disdainful rhythm as he makes his return to the bag, and you will nail him by changing your own rhythm.

The pitcher, if he is not going to be run out of the league by crafty batsmen, has got to learn to field his position well. That means he must play the part of an infielder on bunts or topped balls that come within his reach. He must learn to bend the back and flex the knees—and above all to keep the eyes fastened to the ball—in picking a ball off the ground. Most pitchers nowadays use the very largest glove they can buy. Every now and then during a game a ball will rocket back off the bat straight at the pitcher and about all you can do is fling that big glove up to absorb some of the shock. Sometimes the ball sticks there too.

But most of the balls you field will be balls that must be plucked off the ground and thrown to a base, most often first base. You can use your glove to round these balls up, but get the ball immediately into your bare hand. Do not so much as look at the runner or the base until you see that ball securely in your throwing hand. There are few sorrier sights than the spectacle of a pitcher, with his eye on first base, making several vain grabs at the ball that is almost at his feet, and which he cannot see because he is not looking at it.

When a bunt is expected, the pitcher must come right off the mound after the pitch and advance toward the plate. Two good steps forward will bring you into proper fielding position and then you can move either right or left, depending on which side the ball has gone. If the bunt has gone down the third-base line, then your throw has got to be hurried. You will not have time to straighten up and throw overhand. You will have to sling that ball right from the spot you pick it up, throwing sidearm or even underhand to get the ball to the base ahead of the runner. This is perhaps the play in which there is the most danger that you will look up and fail to take hold of the ball. So school yourself to get right down over the ball, infielder style, and keep your eye on it until you have it in your hand.

On any ground ball hit to your left, you must start fast for first base. Often, you will have the best chance to field the ball. But do not make a project of fielding it. That is, do not swing around to get into good fielding position. Cut straight across the path of the ball. And if you fail to field it, do not chase after it. Keep right on going to first base, because the first baseman will probably be trying for that ball too and someone is going to have to be on the base to make the putout. Never fail to move toward first when the ball goes to your left. This is one of the most important moves you can make. If you fail or forget, the runner is almost sure to be safe.

As you work with your fielders you will have an understanding with them as to just how bunts and ground balls near the mound are to be played. Some first basemen will be able to cover a much wider arc of territory than others. But never leave it up to someone else to get over toward first on a ball to your left. If you are not needed, then you can stay back. But you must get a jump in that direction.

In making a putout at first you will often be cutting straight across the path of the runner, and in danger of a collision. When you are going to get to the base at about the same time as the runner, do not cut him off or charge into him. Instead, hit the second base side of the bag with your foot and keep on going out toward right, parallel to the path of the runner. Pitchers are too costly to risk getting them busted into small pieces on the baselines.

On pop flies near the mound or up the baselines, the fielders should be allowed to make the play, but you will have to take charge most of the time and decide if the catcher or one of the fielders has the best chance. Pick out the man and shout out his name loudly and continually. If one of the other guys fails to hear you—and sometimes a player will concentrate so hard on this play that he will not hear— then you are going to have to move right in and grab the guy who should stay out of it. Hold on to him and keep him from colliding with the other player. A collision with a fully armored catcher may put an infielder right out of the ball game.

The pitcher also has to back up throws, to third, to home, to second, to first. In fact, he should get into every play where he can be of help. To back up a throw properly, you need to be far enough back so the ball won't go over both your heads, or bounce through you both. Stand about twenty-five feet back of the fielder and watch the ball every second. *Always* expect the ball to come to you. In fact, you should always figure that each pitch may roll right back to the mound and you should be ready to field it.

Many pitchers are temperamental, in that they react quickly to all the vicissitudes of the game. But too much "temperament" can spoil a pitcher. If you are the type who is inclined to blow his top at a bad decision, or an error, or a bad break, you will have a hard time on the pitching mound. The moment any pitcher shows signs of being touchy, you can count on having the opposition always "on" him. They will try every way to pull the trigger that sets off the explosion. Because a temper fit weakens a man's confidence. And confidence is one thing a pitcher must never lose. Of course, not every man can be cool and carefree when things are working against him. But a big leaguer has to learn to conceal his temper, to bite back the explosion, and to let himself cool down without any slamming of the glove on the ground, any kicking of the resin bag, or wild shaking of the fists. If you look always fierce, cold, confident, and determined, you will have a psychological edge on the batter.

I realize that there are many good pitchers who are moody, and who resent being taken out of the game. There was a man once who turned and threw the ball at the fence when the manager lifted him. I cannot get sore at a pitcher who wants to stay in and finish the job he started. That is exactly the attitude he should cultivate—the feeling that no matter what the previous batters have done, this *next* guy is going out. But it is still necessary to cultivate an adult attitude toward all the misfortunes that may befall you. Get sore if you like and go into the locker room and kick the furniture or call the manager all the names you like, out of his hearing. But as long as you are on view—and especially in view of the enemy—stay in control of yourself.

Pitchers are often the last ones to realize that they are losing their stuff, for it may seem that just one more pitch will bring it back. Keep telling yourself that no matter what happens, and try to forget about your bad innings or bad days. But do not let success persuade you that you can start to ease up. A pitcher will last longest if he stays in condition the year round, and does not have to fight off sore muscles and flabby flesh every spring. A pitcher should also feed himself a lot of work. There should be hard throwing every day—except the day you pitch and the day immediately after. And if you can keep your legs moving all year round you will be better for it. Run when you can, and run until the sweat pours down. Swimming is good for a steady diet too. And you can keep the throwing muscles limber in the off-season by pulling on chest weights, using the pitching motion.

Pitching is a study too, more so than any other part of the game. There is always something new to learn, about your own skills, or about the hitters you may face. When you are balancing the bench, don't just dream of big salaries and long automobiles. Watch the hitters and baserunners and note their patterns of activity. See what a base-runner does when he is making ready to steal. See what type of pitch a batter will go out on. And at other times, when you are throwing, work on getting control of your extra pitches.

Every pitcher has a few extra tricks going for him. Some work on the "move" to first base until it would take a clairvoyant to detect the difference between that and the real move toward the plate. Some make a habit of "throwing a lot of glove and shoulder" at the batter. That is, as they bring the pitching arm around to make the pitch, they reach the other arm out, with a flicking motion, to help distract the batter. We have a relief pitcher, Stu Miller, who does practically all his pitching with his head and neck. His motions vary so from pitch to pitch that the batter can never tell when the ball is *really* coming. A lot of them will insist that if Stu ever came down with a stiff neck he would be out of a job in two weeks. That is not strictly true, because Stu can still put quite a lot on a baseball. But those twists and gawks and cranings of neck and head add about 50 per cent to his effectiveness.

This brings me to a point that is sometimes ignored. Pitching motions are supposed to be smooth, so the whole strength of the body will be concentrated on the job of pouring that baseball toward the plate. But there is such a thing as a too-smooth motion. If your pitching rhythm is always exactly the same, the hitters will time your pitches almost without trying. Effective pitchers make small changes from time to time if they find that the batters are timing them. They may shorten the windup, or slow down the motion somewhat. Old Satchel Paige used to work a little hesitation into his motion, until he came pretty close to committing a balk. But he was successful for a long time in keeping batters off balance. And keeping them off balance is one of the elements of good pitching.

Take the time therefore to study your own motion and see to it that you do not get into too obvious a groove. Of course, if you are going to make a small change in your motion you must be sure you make it for *all* your pitches, because there are always sharp-eyed observers trying to pick up the small giveaways you may commit— the difference in the way you hold the ball for the curve, the extra deep pump you may make on the fast ball. Often you will outwit these readers just by keeping the ball in your glove, out of sight, as you take the sign, and keep it hidden in your glove until you pitch it. Some pitchers do give pitches away when they expose the ball in their pitching hand, particularly when they hold the seams one way for the fast ball and another way for the curve.

In working with your catcher, you have to remember that, while you are certainly in charge of the baseball and must use the pitch you want to use, he may know something about this particular hitter that you do not know, or may have noticed something that has escaped you. So if he gets persistent when you brush off a sign, call him out and talk about it. And naturally you will make extra sure that you both understand the signs completely. You may have an agreement that a brush-off means you will use the opposite of what has been called for—the fast ball instead of the curve or vice versa. Or you may want to use a fake brush-off, just to add to the batter's confusion, when you think he is guessing with you. These are matters that require complete mutual understanding. And, like most other refinements, they are best worked out through playing ball games, which is the only real way to learn any part of the game.

13. It's a long time since I pitched a major league ball game. But I always held my fast ball wih my fingertips across the seams.

14. Completing my pitching delivery, I would land with knees bent and feet parallel, ready to field the ball if it came back to me.

15. The curve ball delivery is made by turning the hand over as you bring it down. The ball is released from between the thumb and forefinger.

16. You throw the slider just as you might throw a football, cutting the hand down and away at just about this height.

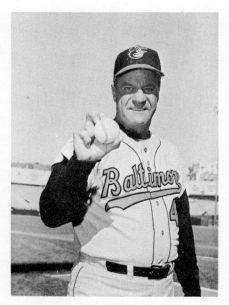

17. The knuckle ball is held in the fingertips, with the hand behind the ball. This gets the ball off without any spin.

18. The sinker is thrown by turning the hand inward as it is released, from about this height. The index finger supplies most of the pressure.

◎

THE FIRST BASEMAN

The first baseman can make his job big or small, depending on his own skills. There have been big league first basemen who seemed to limit the sphere of their activity to an area about the size of a silver dollar. And there have been others who have ranged far to the right and left, have charged right down the batter's throat, and have sprinted into right field to take fly balls away from the outfielder. Many clubs have carried first basemen who contributed not much more than their bats. But these are not the men you want to model yourself after. An ably-fielding first baseman can take a lot of runs away from the opposition and tighten up the whole infield.

Not too long ago, they taught first basemen to try to catch all balls with two hands. But that was before the trapper-style mitt was perfected. Now, as Casey Stengel puts it, the first baseman plays jai alai. He takes everything one-handed in that big scoop, which actually puts an extension of several inches on his hand. Even pop flies are often caught one-handed, because the big leather basket most first basemen use does not lend itself to two-handed catches.

But the major task of the first baseman remains the same. He must know all the time where the base is in relation to his feet and he must be able to get one foot on the base quickly, without stumbling around, so he can make the putout. When you practice any part of first-base play, you should always have a base to work around, even if it is no more than a square drawn in the dirt. This way you will develop the proper instinct for getting to the base quickly and directly.

Most of your job of course will be concerned with catching the throws to make the putout. Whenever a ball is hit that may lead to a play at first base, you must move quickly to the bag. Don't ever make an infielder wait for you to show up to take his throw. Get over there and be waiting for it. And before the throw comes make sure you know exactly where the bag is in relation to your feet. You can't afford to take time to look for the bag after the throw is in the air, or in your glove. You do not position your foot on the bag, nor do you stretch out toward the fielder until *after* the throw is on its way. If you commit yourself to a certain position and the throw is off target, you will waste time getting untangled. So the stance you take as you await the throw will have to anticipate a bad throw. *Never* assume that the throw will be perfect. Take a position on the inside edge of the bag, the second-base edge. Look down at the bag at once so you will know just where it is. Then stand, knees bent, arms loose and away from your body, and watch the man who fields the ball. As soon as the ball is on its way, get your foot on the bag and *stretch* toward the ball. Put your *toe* on the bag. If you try to keep contact with your heel, your stretch may pull your foot right off the bag and result in your missing your putout. The purpose of your stretch is to shorten the distance between you and the man who throws the ball. Obviously, the sooner you get the ball, the better chance you will have of putting out the runner, so you get just as much length out of your stretch as you can, striding just as far as your legs will let you and reaching the full length of your arm. Your standard stretch, if you are left-handed, will be with your left foot on the bag (so you can get that glove hand out as far as it will go) and your right leg striding toward the ball. (While all good first basemen are not left-handers by any means, first base is the *only* position a left-handed ballplayer can play without extreme awkwardness.)

If the throw is off target (and remember you expect *every* throw will be) then you must be prepared to jump into a position to snag the throw and make the putout. This may mean shifting your feet on the base, making contact with right foot instead of left, so as to be able to reach the throw. You have to be agile and confident about shifting this way, and that means knowing at all times *exactly* where the bag is. You develop this agility and confidence only through practice, and no amount of study will give you the skill if you do not put in long hours playing first base, with someone throwing to you.

Many throws to first base will be in the dirt. These you will have to dig right out as if they were batted balls, getting your head down over the ball and taking it out in front. Actually the short-hop balls you will find easiest to field. The ones that may trouble you may be the ones that hit far out in front and take a long skip into you, so concentrate on this type as you practice. But try always to field the throw out in front.

Really wild throws will pull you right off the base, for it is better to keep the ball from going through, even if you have to concede the base to the runner. And sometimes you can even get back in time with the ball to make the out. But some throws that are just a bit wild may still be handled properly if you have confidence enough. If the ball is on the base but still far over your head, you can sometimes bring it down just by hopping back into foul territory, with your forward toe on the foul-line edge of the bag. The extra distance you allow may be just enough to enable you to reach the ball.

The really rough putout at first base, as everyone knows, is the throw that pulls you right into the runner. There is always a temptation to try to take this behind the baseline. But the proper way is to reach right down toward the runner, cool and confident, and take it right in front of the line, even if you pluck it right out of his chest. Then a quick hop will get your feet out of his way and make the putout. If the throw is far down the line toward home go down inside the line after it. Sometimes you can tag the runner as he goes by.

A good first baseman, who is not just pastured at first to keep his bat in the lineup, goes after any ball he can reach, and stays with it unless and until some other fielder calls him off it. You will of course play the batters in accordance with their habits and with the tactical situation. Left-handed hitters will almost always need to be played well behind the baseline, unless there is a runner to be kept on, or unless a bunt is obvious. The pitcher will have the job of covering first base if a ground ball pulls you far from the bag. Your job will be to get the ball to him in such a way as to make it easy for him to put the runner out. To do this, you try to feed him the ball, nice and easy, when he is still a few steps away from the bag, so he will not have to catch the ball and look for the bag all at the same time. Do not wait for him to get on the bag, or you will be placing him in danger of a full-speed collision with the runner. Let him have the ball before he gets to the base, when he is still far enough away so he can take the moment needed to find the bag and get his foot on it. But do not let the pitcher make the putout if you field the ball close enough to the bag to make the putout yourself. *Always* make the putout when you can because the less your pitcher has to run during the ball game the longer he will last. But if you must toss the ball to the pitcher, be sure he can see it all the way. Do not hide it behind your glove, or flip it under your arm. Pull your glove hand out of the way and put the ball in the air as you move toward the bag. Face the pitcher directly as you throw to him.

A left-hander has a big advantage at first because he is facing the play most of the time. He can pick up a bunt and fire it to second base without having to turn around or twist his body awkwardly. On the 3–6–3 double play, he can make his throw to second naturally, facing right at the bag. This is a pretty play but it is not really a difficult one and requires only practice at keeping the throw off the baseline so it will not hit the runner, and in scrambling back to accept the return throw. What makes it difficult occasionally is the return throw, which frequently has to be made right over a sliding runner, so the first baseman must not only be swift in returning to cover the bag but must be agile in taking throws that are hurried and sometimes off target.

A right-handed first baseman who must make a throw to second from down the first-base line usually does best to turn all the way around to get the throw off. This will provide him more momentum than the awkward twist and throw that would be necessary otherwise. The time lost in the turn will be made up in the speed of the throw. On the double play throw, however, from between first and second base, a flat-footed throw is best because it is necessary to get it off fast. The body twist, to get the arm into throwing position, will pull the left knee right to the ground. But a quick snap will get the ball down the short distance in good time. Then you must scramble to get back to the bag. You have no time to watch to see how your throw was handled.

When a bunt is expected, the first baseman must move quickly toward the plate as the pitcher starts to pitch. Make sure you *know* he is coming to the plate with the ball and is not going to throw to first to keep the runner close. Then sprint hard for the plate. If you can pick up the bunted ball immediately, you may be able to get the runner at second, and this is the play you must always look for if you field the bunt cleanly. You must get hold of the ball first, however, and you can do this best by using both hands on it, the gloved hand to round it up and the bare hand to lay hold of it. When you have it solidly in your throwing hand, look to second and see if you have a chance for the runner.

You won't have time to study the situation. A quick glance will have to tell you the answer to two questions: Will the throw beat the runner? Is there someone there to take the throw? If you see you can't make the out at second, fire the ball down fast to first base, *inside* the baseline. If you have to take several steps to pick up the bunt, or if you fumble it badly, you are not going to get the lead runner. Go to first for the sure out instead. Sometimes the pitcher will try to field the bunt. You still must keep coming to back him up, because if he misses his stab at it, he is going to go for first base to take your throw.

The actual fielding of ground balls we can discuss later, when we talk of infield play in general. The special jobs of the first baseman, besides those already outlined, include fielding pop fouls down the line and acting as cutoff man on throws from right field to home plate. The catcher is going to go after the fouls between first and home, but the first baseman has got to try for those he can reach, or thinks he can reach. But if he is called off, he must leave the job to the catcher, although he should stay near on the chance he may be able to rescue a muffed ball before it falls. On pop flies over the first baseman's head and down the right-field line, the second baseman usually has a better line on the ball, from not having to turn around to get the proper angle. Let him take all of these that are in his reach. Those near the stand and toward home plate will be yours. Take them one-handed if you prefer, as you probably will. But make it a practice to catch pop flies rather high, so you may have a second chance if you fail to hold the ball tight.

When there is going to be a play at home on a ball hit to right field, the first baseman is often the cutoff man and must position himself so he can grab the ball and make a play at second base, or even third base, if there is a chance of getting the runner there. You cannot do this effectively if you are too close to your own bag when you make the cutoff, for then you will be unable to see what the baserunners are doing. Move far enough down the line toward home so that you can keep the runner or runners in your line of sight and can make a throw to second or third, without having to turn completely around.

The first baseman gets many a line drive in his direction when left-handers are batting. You can often make the out on these even if you do not catch them on the fly. So if you flag one down, do not waste time cursing your luck. Scramble after the ball and beat the runner to the bag. The pitcher will be sprinting to first to cover and you can make the toss to him or, if the play was close to the bag, you can very possibly beat the runner there.

Your territory extends as far up toward second base as you can cover. If a hot ground ball heads for the hole between you and the second baseman, do not back off to let the second baseman have it. Try for anything you can reach, particularly if you can make the play in front of the second baseman.

19. Coach Billy Hunter never did wear his glove this way, but this is Boog Powell's glove and Boog likes to keep one finger outside. He puts adhesive tape on the glove where his finger rides. The first baseman's glove is worn on the fingertips. Casey Stengel says that modern first basemen "play jai alai," because they catch the ball in a scoop.

20. But Billy, wearing his glove in the old way, advises trying to catch *throws* in two hands whenever possible. Here he shows how the first baseman stretches for a throw. Notice that the whole foot is on the base, so that it will not be pulled away by the stretch.

Billy, playing first base, takes a ...ow in the big glove, with the ...at hand there to make sure he ...ngs onto it.

22. When the first baseman holds a runner on, he stands at the inside corner of the bag, the home-plate side, with one foot in foul ground. He holds the glove up as a target for the pitcher.

23. In tossing a ball to the pitcher, when the pitcher has to cover first, the first baseman must be sure to pull his glove out of the way so the pitcher can see the ball.

...4. Then the first baseman tosses the ball underhand ... the *pitcher* (not to the bag), trying to get it to the ...tcher a few steps before the pitcher reaches the ...ase.

25. When the first baseman fields a ground ball, he gets his glove right down into the dirt to smother the ball, then grabs it with his bare hand.

◎

PLAYING THE INFIELD

Second base, third base, and shortstop are somewhat less specialized than first base, most of the outs being tagouts, and there being not so many difficult throws to handle. But all infielders must field ground balls aggressively, moving in on them every time if possible, and trying always to field the ball well out in front of the body. An infielder cannot be afraid of the dirt. He must get down into it, take his stance with knees well-flexed and back bent to bring him as near to the ground as he can get and still be comfortable and able to move in any direction. The weight should be well forward, as the first move should always be *toward* the ball. The feet should be comfortably spread, the wrists limber, and the arms relaxed and the hands out in front. Never get yourself locked into a position with your elbows inside your spread knees. That will make it difficult for you to get a proper start to either side.

Fielding ground balls is, of course, a matter of endless practice, to train the hands to react instinctively to the action of the ball. But you should tell yourself from the start that you are going to go get the ball. Do not wait for it or try to adjust to its bounce. Charge right in and smother it out in front of your feet. It is important to learn to keep the head down—down—down. Get it down so near the ball that you can see your own cap bill in front of you. That is the way to make sure you adjust to any sort of bounce. If you flinch, if you turn your head to one side, if you lift your chin to take a look at the base you are going to throw to, you will be unable to adjust to an erratic hop. Actually you are far more likely to get hit by the ball if you take your eyes away from it than if you keep your head down and your eyes right on the ball.

There will be ground balls that just explode at you so fast you can do no more than fall back half a step and grab them. But these will be the exceptions, and will announce themselves to you before you can charge them. Tell yourself you are going to charge every ball. If it is well to the right or left, do not back off to round it up. Cut right across its path and smother it. The easiest bounce to play is the short hop, when the ball is just leaving the ground. Experience will enable you to speed up or slow down your approach to a ground ball so that you can get it on that hop, right close to the ground. Get your hands down into the dirt to field it. If it takes a sudden unexpected hop, you will adjust to it automatically. Just do not let the ball play you. That is, do not wait for it to reach you on a hop that is easy to handle. That hop may never come. And do not sidle up to the ball, to take it as it goes by. There will be some, of course, that you will have to stab at on one side or another. But your aim should always be to get to the ball fast and get your body in front of it. Sometimes you will have to take a big hop, to keep from making a crossover step, and to land squarely in front of the ball. But as long as you bear in mind that you must operate close to the ground, with knees and back bent, and with arms out front, you will learn how to adjust yourself to anything that comes your way.

The most difficult balls to field will be those that come straight at you. It is harder to judge the speed and bounce of these and you will find yourself, as you start, often fooled by these. So it is best to get plenty of practice on them, to work on charging them hard and meeting them out in front of your feet. You can field these in your normal stride, with one foot ahead of the other. But your hands should reach out farther than your front foot.

Infield pop flies are actually more difficult to deal with than outfield flies. An outfielder can afford to keep his eye on a ball hit over his head and watch it over his shoulder as he retreats. But an infielder does best, when a ball goes over his head, to turn and sprint for the place where he judges the ball will come down. Then he can look back and line it up. The worst way to try to play one of these balls is to back-pedal beneath it. You will have to back up sometimes on balls that at first seem about to fall in front of you. But do not try to move backward to get under a ball hit well beyond you. If there is a strong wind, try to position yourself so the wind will bring the ball toward you. It is always easier to adjust to those than to the balls that are suddenly blown out of your reach. When the ball is one that an outfielder is going to try for, and you have it lined up well, you must shout that you are going to take it. Say it loud and often: "I've got it! I've got it!" And wave other fielders away with both hands. An outfielder moving in at full speed can really do damage if he bumps into you.

Your throw to first base after fielding a ball should be made overhand if you can possibly manage it. You do not always have time to straighten up and throw the ball from over your shoulder, but many times you do. And the speed of the throw makes up for some of the split seconds lost in straightening up. On slow rollers and bunts and high hoppers, with a fast man going down to first, you have to get the throw off as best you can. Of course you charge such balls to get to them without wasting time. But when you get hold of the ball you often have to let it fly from wherever you picked it up, and that means an underhand sling from right off the ground, or a sidearm throw from your hip, and sometimes a snap throw from midair. Just be sure you face the target when you throw and get all the strength you can spare into the effort. Overhand throws look better to the first baseman because they do not curve or sink the way other throws sometimes do.

Infielders should always practice around bases, or around imaginary bases, so that the position of the bag in relation to the play is always in the back of the mind. And infielders should make a habit of getting into every play where they can be of any help. An infielder never waits to be told a ball is his. Everything he can reach is his. And when he cannot reach a ball, he can often back up the play, or just be handy in case of an error or a bad hop. Good infielders habitually back up throws, even throws from catcher to pitcher when men are on base.

Every infielder will have a chance to act as relay man on throws from the deep outfield at one time or another. This is a job that requires alertness and team play. A relay man should never be blind to what is happening on the diamond. If he does not know what to do with the ball when he gets it, he is just in the way. He will run out on the grass to take the throw from the outfielder—to make the outfielder's throw as short as possible. And he will wave his arms over his head so the outfielder can pick him up without looking for him. But he must also keep one eye on the diamond, which means he cannot turn his back completely on the play. He should stand sideways between outfielder and infield so that when the throw comes in he will know at once whether he can nail the runner at home or has a chance for a runner at some other base. There are not many things more stupid-looking than a relay man standing with the baseball in his fist, not knowing where to throw it.

All infielders have to tag baserunners, too, and this is not always as simple a job as it may sound. The baserunner is going to be trying to avoid your tag and may even be trying to scare you out of putting the ball on him. As in fielding a grounder, you have to get your head right over a tag play. Because there is no telling which way a runner may slide—either to the right or left of the base to avoid a tag—your best position for making a tagout is to straddle the bag. Hold the ball securely in both hands and as the runner comes in, get the ball right down between the bag and his incoming leg or foot, so he *must* slide into it. Never try to tag him on the body as he slides, because then his foot may be on the bag before you touch him. Make the tag with the ball in both hands and with the back of the glove turned toward the runner. You will usually find this play is perfectly safe, but just in case you do get tangled with the runner's spikes, you will do better to take them in the back of the wrist than on the tender flesh on the inside of the wrist.

Going to meet low throws is another good habit to get into. The relay or the cutoff man should get the ball fairly high, so as to be able to get a throw off quickly. If the ball is coming low, then you should hustle out to meet it so you can get it about shoulder height. If it comes too high, you can give ground until it will reach you at the proper height. But if you are not relaying you can still help by backing up the man who is—provided of course that you are not leaving a base—and especially not third base—uncovered. Throws from the outfield do sometimes go over the head of the relay man, and a backup man can then frequently make a putout, because baserunners, seeing a wild throw from the outfield, have a tendency to run more recklessly.

It is in the infield that tight team play pays off best. Every infielder should be ready to take over any job that needs to be done. If the man who is supposed to act as relay man has failed to get out there, then *you* get out. If the pitcher has forgotten to back up third base on a throw, then *you* back it up. And if the catcher has had to go far back of the plate to catch a foul with a man on base, and the pitcher has moved in to the plate, the shortstop is ordinarily supposed to get in by the pitcher's mound to relay a possible throw from the catcher to second base. If the shortstop forgets, *you* get in there and be ready to relay. An infielder is better than a pitcher at snap throws.

While you have to get plenty of practice at fielding ground balls and especially at putting away pop flies under all sorts of conditions, you ought to work out as much as possible with other infielders, so that you will develop the habit of working together, will learn to judge just when to feed a throw to a teammate who is approaching base for a putout, and just what sort of throws to expect from the others. Also you should always be conscious of the need to throw to a base every time you field a ball. You have to become accurate on every type of throw and you need far more practice than you will get in just playing the regular ball games. You can always chisel a little extra practice in fielding by stationing yourself in the infield during batting practice. A hit off a pitched ball is a great deal better practice than a fungo hit.

Infielders do not always have to have great speed, although a real slowboat may have a hard time holding up his end of the job. But an infielder must be alert, with quick reactions, and with a great willingness to get into the play. As he takes his position in the field, his weight forward, his eyes on the ball (or on the batter), his knees and back bent, he should expect and *want* every pitch to be hit to him. When a ball is popped into the air, he should *want* to make the catch—and should try to make it, too, unless he is called off it by a better-positioned fielder. Reluctance to move right or left after a ball because it "belongs" to someone else will soon disqualify a man for the infield. There is no time for protocol when a ground ball is sizzling through the infield. The man who can get to it first is the man it belongs to. And if he misses it, there should be someone nearby who can retrieve it, should it bounce his way.

Nowadays all infielders use gloves not unlike the trap the first baseman uses. They are extra big and usually extra stiff, to keep balls from skipping through them. Many fielders like to wear them with one finger outside the glove to ease the pounding of hard throws, just the way most catchers do. But no matter how you wear yours you should not hesitate to get it down into the dirt after a ground ball. I do not mean you have to sprawl in the dirt or make headlong dives after balls that you have no hope of reaching. I mean you should *dig* those ground balls out, even if you bring part of the infield up with them. Don't try to be dainty about it. Don't give the ball a chance to roll under your hands. Reach out there and smother it on the ground. Even if you don't grab it securely the first time, if you stop it, you always have a chance for the putout. As a matter of fact, a fumbled ball or a dropped throw should always be pounced on. Sometimes they work better than if the misplay had not been made, for they occasionally tempt a runner, who has been hesitating, to try for an extra base, and a quick play may put him out. Infielders therefore have no time to shake their heads over errors. A good infielder is after any missed ball like a terrier, and ready always to throw it where it will do the most good. Of course it sometimes does the most good to hang onto the ball. You must always look at the base to find your target and to see what your chances are of making a play. If there is no chance, *hold* the ball! Carry it back to the pitcher if you like, but don't send it flying uselessly around the infield. Alert runners like nothing better than to draw throws, because every throw is a potential error.

26. When the pitcher has released the ball toward the plate, the infielder, with his eye on the ball, is right up on his toes, ready to charge in on a ground ball.

27. When he fields the ball he has his knees bent and his back bent and his head right down over the ball. He tries to field every ball out in front.

28. The head stays down and eyes are on the ball until it is safely held in the bare hand. Only then is the infielder ready to sight the target he is going to throw to.

◎

THE SECOND BASEMAN

Sometimes it seems that every play a second baseman makes has to be an awkward one. He is almost always, either back to the play or side-wise to it, and throwing across his body or snapping the ball off with one knee on the ground. So it takes a good man to operate in this position. A strong arm is not so vital as it would be to a shortstop or third baseman. But quickness, confidence, and courage are essential. The second baseman covers a wide section of dirt and a whole lot of grass and he is always on the move. He must be ready to charge in on the grass if a drag bunter finds him playing back too far. He must range down to cover first base if the first baseman and pitcher are covering a bunt. He must sprint to the edge of the stands to take foul flies that go over the first baseman's head, and he must also take short flies in center and right fields. All this in addition to covering his "normal" position between first and second, and making tag plays and forceouts on the bag.

With a left-handed batter up, the second baseman is the key opera-tor. If the man is fast, and a good bunter, the second baseman may even have to cheat a little—move in toward the baseline to be ready to charge a drag bunt. If the ball goes up the middle, the second baseman must cut it off if he can. If it gets by the first baseman, he must try to recover it. Many times, his throws will be hurried and off balance. From the direction of first base, he can often turn all the way around after fielding a ball, so as to get power and speed enough on his throw to second. But a ball that must be thrown to first is often thrown sidearm, right across the chest, without any time to straighten up. It is best of course to straighten up, face the bag directly, and throw overhand. But when the ball is moving slowly, and the runner is moving faster than the ball, as frequently happens, then the pickup and throw must be almost in the same motion. This is a play that needs lots of extra practice, because it is difficult to achieve accuracy on this throw. Of course, these emergency-type throws must not be made when there is time to do better. But at second base there is not always a lot of time.

There is even less time when a double play must be made. Then the throw is sometimes an underhand toss, even a sort of scoop with the glove, or a flat-footed twist and throw that brings one knee to the ground. But here again, the baseman should always use the best throw he can and not hustle the throw when there is no need. The shortstop will be the pivot man when the ground ball comes to the second baseman, unless the ball has been fielded so close to the bag that it is possible for the second baseman to make the forceout himself. Practicing together will enable the second-base combination to work out the system that best suits their own speed and skills. But there are some basic points to remember: Be sure not to conceal the ball from your partner when you get set to throw it to him. Unless there is a really desperate hurry, get the ball in your bare hand to throw it. The scoop and toss with the glove is a risky performance. Pull your left arm and glove out of the way, so the other man can see the ball. Feed it to him chest high, so he will be able to get his throw off fast. Face him directly as you make the toss and move toward the bag.

When the ball is fielded well down the line toward first, a snap throw will be needed. The second baseman will be awkwardly positioned for the throw. He may be able to shift his feet with one quick hop, so as to face the bag and be able to get off an overhand throw. But most of the good second basemen I have seen like to make this throw flat-footed, with a quick twist of the body to get the right arm back into throwing position, and with one knee dipping to the ground. Of course the ball should still go to the pivot man chest high. Then he can make the forceout and get the relay throw off without wasted motion.

When the second baseman acts as pivot man on the double play he has several different ways of performing. The play-safe way, and the one I would probably recommend in school baseball, where double plays are not very common, is the one in which the second baseman tags the base with his left foot and then shoves back off the base in the outfield direction and makes his throw from outside the baseline. This is not so efficient as the big-league method, but it avoids collisions and lessens the chance of throwing the ball into the runner.

Another method is to take the throw on the right-field side of the base, then step right across second base, dragging the foot over the base to make the out, and firing the ball to first from the infield side of the bag. There are times, of course, when the throw and runner reach base at almost the same time and you have to release your throw right over his head. He will be trying to "take you out" on this play and you must be practiced at getting rid of the ball fast, while jumping high enough to get your shins out of his way. There is one thing the second baseman must concentrate on in this play, and that is turning to face first base squarely. As usual, the second baseman will come into this play with his back to the action, and he must turn squarely around to insure the accuracy of his throw. If it is not going to be possible to get off a good strong throw, then it is better to be satisfied with the one sure out.

The shortstop and second baseman should work out between them a simple sign to indicate who will cover the bag when a hit-and-run is expected—that is, when it seems likely that the runner will go on the pitch and the hitter will try to hit behind him. (This happens most often in a close game, with one out and a man on first who is not too fast a runner.) In this situation, or when a steal is expected, and it is decided the second baseman will cover the bag, the baseman can cheat a little toward the base so as to get there a split second sooner. A steal, of course, will mean a tag play, and the baseman should straddle the bag and *wait* for the throw. Even if the throw is less than perfect, you should let it come to you and not leave the bag for it unless it really is going to be wild. Keep your knees bent and your arms loose and your hands out in front of you, ready to reach for the throw once you can see where it is coming. Even if you have to dig it out of the gravel it may still be possible to lay the tag on the runner, so don't abandon your post until you *know* the throw is going to be too far off target. As in any such situation, you must always expect a bad throw and be relaxed and ready to move.

The double steal presents the second baseman with an additional problem. When there is a runner on third, the baseman must keep that runner in his sights even while he is awaiting the throw. If the runner on third takes off for home before the throw reaches you, the thing to do is abandon the other runner completely and run right into the diamond to meet the throw, then hammer it back to the catcher. Far better to cut off that run than to cut down the runner at second. You may even work out a signal you can exchange with the catcher to indicate that you will come in for the throw and try for the man on third. You cannot get both men on this play. If you make the play at second, the man on third is going to score, assuming he has started before the throw reaches you. But if you outguess him with this signal, you can cut him down or get him hung up on the baseline.

When there is a three-and-two count on the batter, with a man on first, there is always a good chance the runner will be going down to second on the pitch. In this situation too, you cheat a little bit toward the bag and break for it just as soon as you see the pitch has gone by the batter and struck him out. You must be sure to be on the bag as soon as the catcher is ready to throw. Otherwise that runner is certain to be safe.

The man who can best work a pickoff play when there is a runner on second base is the shortstop, but the second baseman can help keep the runner close (if you want to keep him close) by making bluff starts for second when the pitcher has the ball and the runner is getting too bold. Once in a hundred times you may even beat the runner to the bag and get a quick throw from the pitcher. But if there is a pickoff play on, with the shortstop trying to edge a little closer to the bag than the runner before starting his count, you do not want to interfere by scaring the runner back.

While you cannot deliberately stand in a runner's path on the baseline if you do not have the ball, you do have a right to field a ball on the baseline. You do not need to get out of the runner's way if you are making a legitimate try for the ball. If he runs into you and prevents you from fielding a ball or catching a fly, he is out for interference.

I think a second baseman needs more practice at his position than any other fielder, because of the difficulty of the throws. You should work out on ground balls with a baseman on your left to throw to and give extra attention to the slow-rolling ball that comes right at you—the one that you must charge fast, pick up cleanly, and throw without any wasted motion. Believe me, you cannot make this play with stiff legs or a straight back. You have to scoot in like a terrier, and smother that ball well out in front. This means getting right close to the turf, so you could eat the ball if you wanted to. A second baseman who does not get his hands, even his elbows, into the dirt, is not doing his job.

29. When the second baseman throws to the shortstop to start a double play, he does not always have time to turn and face the target squarely, so he pivots to his right to get his throwing arm back and snaps the ball straight to the shortstop.

30. The shortstop takes the throw as he approaches second base. It should hit him about shoulder high.

32. He faces first base directly, points his toe at the target, and fires the ball down from *outside* the baseline.

31. The shortstop makes the out by dragging his toe across the base. He holds the ball in his bare hand, ready to relay it down to first base.

33. On a tag play, the baseman straddles the bag as he awaits the throw.

34. The baseman gets the ball in his *bare* hand before he makes the tag and holds his position astraddle the bag as the runner slides in.

35. To make the tag, the baseman still holds the ball in his bare hand, protects it with his glove, and turns the *back* of his glove toward the runner. He puts the ball down where the runner must slide into it.

36. When the second baseman acts as pivot man on a double play, he makes the out just as the shortstop did. But then he steps to the *inside* of the baseline, faces first base squarely, and throws down. There are other ways of making this play, but this is the big-league method.

◎

THE SHORTSTOP

—————

A glove man who really wants to enjoy the game should play shortstop. In this spot you get every kind of chance, from sizzling ground balls to sky-high pops or high fouls along the left-field rail. You are the real playmaker on pickoffs, on relays, on double steals, on double plays. You throw long and you throw short. You make tagouts on steals. Sometimes you even pass the catcher's signs along to the third baseman and to the outfield. And you have the infield action right in front of you at all times.

A strong arm and lots of agility are indispensable in a shortstop because he has to make many a throw to first from deep in the hole near third base and also has to flag down the ground balls that streak up the middle. He must be able to move with equal speed and confidence in either direction and make stops on either side of his body. The position in the far distant days—before I ever heard of the game and even before Casey Stengel—was called short-stop because the fielder was a sort of caddy to the pitcher, playing almost behind him and picking up the balls the pitcher could not stop. But for a whole lifetime now the shortstop has been expected to play deep behind the baseline, and for this reason many of his throws really come from the short outfield. There have been games when the shortstop has not had a single fielding chance. (Frankie Crosetti played such a game in 1940.) But there has never been a game when the shortstop has not seen plenty of action, in relaying throws from the outfield, taking throws from the catcher, or scurrying around behind a baserunner to keep him from getting too good a start. A shortstop on that account has to keep his wheels in good shape, and he cannot afford to grow fat.

The shortstop is moving in on almost all ground balls that come his way. He has to play well back to keep the ground balls from skipping by, but he cannot get so far back that he will be too far away to throw the runner out. So when you take over this job you have to figure out just where you can play so that you will be able to get to all the ground balls—and most of them, what with all the right-handed batters in the game, will be near your position—and still be able to power that ball over on a line to the first baseman fast enough to beat the best runners. Balls through the middle, and even slightly to the other side of second base can be reached by the second baseman often. But it is still better if you take them. They will be on your glove-hand side and so can be fielded with less awkwardness, and you will be moving in the right direction—*toward* first—to get off a faster and more accurate throw.

But the one thing that the shortstop must learn to do is charge the ground balls. While plenty of hot shots will come at you here that won't give you a chance to do more than get your glove into position, you should still be poised at all times with your weight forward and should move in hard on every ground ball you see. A runner can reach base safely on a ball that bounds high and lazy over the pitcher's mound, or that trickles out on the grass past the mound, if you do not charge in and grab it. Waiting for the right bounce or swinging out to round up the ball can give the runner all the time he needs to beat your throw to first. Your concern then should be to cut right across the path of every ball to right or left, and to move right in on top of the ones that come straight at you. Naturally you will be down there with knees and back bent and head over the ball. But you will straighten up to throw overhand most of the time. The sidearm and off-balance throws are the desperation throws to be used only when you have had to come a long way after the ball and have only a split second to beat the runner. An overhand throw is easier to handle even when it is not right on target. It bounces more cleanly and it does not dip or curve, so there are fewer chances for error.

The shortstop will often be the one to take the throw on a steal, and the same advice goes for him as I gave to the second baseman. Get astraddle the bag and *wait* for that throw. Expect a bad throw, but do not give up on the runner unless the throw is going to be too far off target for you to be in a position to make the tag.

The shortstop will be more often asked to play the relay man on throws from the outfield because he is supposed to have a better arm than the second baseman. Many times you will be called on to throw to a base from well out on the outfield grass. If you play the position properly, you will not have to look around to find out where the runner is, because you will have had him in the corner of your eye right along. But no matter where he is, do not throw to a base until you know there is someone there to get the throw. Perhaps the baseman has been backing you up and is still scrambling to get to the bag. You do not throw to the base, but to the fielder. You either wait for him to get into position to make the tag, or, if it is a forceout, you feed him the ball when he is two or three strides away from the base, so he can have it with him while he looks for the base.

The shortstop is the best man to put on the sign for the pickoff play, in which the pitcher, after taking his position on the mound, turns and fires the ball to pick off the runner at second base. Your job here is to try to get closer to the base than the runner is. If you get into that position, you make a sign to the pitcher. You both then begin to count, silently in some rhythm that you have practiced together. At the count of two, you break full speed for second base. At the count of three, he turns and throws to the base, *knowing* you will be there. If you cannot get closer to the base than the runner is, you can at least make him cut down his lead by bluffing him back. And if he fails to get back quickly after the pitch, you can scramble for the bag to take a throw from the catcher.

There is lots of backup work for the shortstop. He often backs up the third baseman on ground balls. If he is not acting as relay man, he will back up the relay man. If he is not taking the throw at second, he can back that up. And with men on base he can back up the pitcher on throws from the catcher. The shortstop is best situated to do the hollering in the infield. He can see almost all that goes on, including the signs from the catcher, and he can even have voice signals to tell the other basemen when they can be ready for a certain type of blow. If a tight pitch has been called for on a right-handed batter, the third baseman may want to cheat a bit toward the baseline. Or if it is an outside pitch, the second baseman may want to adjust to the possibility of the ball's coming on his side of the diamond. But shifts of this sort should not be made too soon.

There are plenty of hitters crafty enough to make note of such a shift and use it for a tipoff on what the pitcher will throw.

On my club my shortstop happens to be the man who probably knows the most baseball of anyone (including the manager) on the Baltimore payroll, and he does a good deal more than simply play his position. He is quick to tell a rookie outfielder where to play a certain hitter. He injects pop into the infield with his chatter. And he will walk in to help a pitcher slow himself down a little, or even share some of his own knowledge of what the enemy manager may be up to. Not every shortstop is equipped to do that. But it is good to have an aggressive, talk-it-up type in that position because he can actually captain a lot of the plays and help keep the infield alert. If he and the pitchers can develop a good pickoff play, they can kill off a lot of eager baserunners. And if he learns to keep his eye on the runners when he is acting as relay man, he can choke off many a rally by chopping down a runner before he can score.

◎

THE THIRD BASEMAN

No infielder can play championship baseball and be a slow thinker. But the third baseman has to be more than just a fast thinker. He has to be a lightning thinker. That is because plays develop so fast at his corner, because hit balls reach him in such a hurry, and because there always seems one more play to be made after a play at third. I know it has always been traditional to say that a third baseman has got to have a strong arm, because of the long, hard throw he must make to first. And it is true that most third basemen have been able to throw hard. Some have even turned into pitchers. But more important than strength is what the football players call "quick release"— the ability to get rid of that ball in a tearing hurry. Brooks Robinson does not have a really outstandingly strong arm. But I don't believe I ever saw anyone who gets rid of a ball any faster than he can. His reactions are fast as a rattlesnake's and his throw takes off almost before he has cocked his arm.

At this position, there are many many throws that must be made without straightening up. Bunts and slow rollers, because of the distance to first base, usually have to be picked up and fired to first in the same motion. So a third baseman has got to be ready to move toward the plate with every pitch that is made. He usually plays two or three strides deeper than the base, and many third basemen start moving toward the plate every time the pitcher throws there. This is not absolutely necessary, as long as you keep your weight well forward and get right on your toes ready to move with each pitch. You will, of course, like all the infielders, be playing with your knees deeply flexed and your back bent—and your eyes fixed either on the baseball or on the hitter. Once in a while, when there is a man on third in a tight game, it is necessary to play right on a line with the bag. And believe me, when you are in that position a well-hit ball by a right-hander can come at you like a jet. A third baseman needs plenty of courage on that account. He has got to stick in there like a bulldog, and not give ground on any sort of drive. The balls that come so fast can be knocked down and still picked up to make the out at first. But you have to have the guts to get your body on a line with the ball and bring it to a stop. Of course, there are times when the best you can do is stretch out full length and get the glove in the way. But one thing you never do is retreat.

A third baseman fields everything he can reach. It goes without saying, of course, that everything on his right has to be fielded by him —or else it will go to the left fielder. But he should cut off anything on his left that he can possibly reach. If one gets by, the shortstop may get it. But nothing should be left for the shortstop if there is any chance that the third baseman can field it—except that pop flies into short left are usually best handled by the shortstop, who can approach them from a better angle.

If the batter bunts down the third-base line, the third baseman is usually the only man who can make the play—unless the bunt is short enough for the catcher. If it is right on the line, the best thing to do is let it roll in the hope it will go foul. When it does, of course you sweep it right away with your glove, so it won't trickle back again. But if it is on the grass, you are probably going to have to charge in, pick up the ball in your bare hand, and sling it to first without straightening your back. To do this you have to keep your eye right on the ball every moment, until you have it tight in your throwing hand. This is a Fancy Dan play, but it must not be done carelessly. If you look up from the ball to sight the target, the chances are very good that you will come up with a handful of air.

Of course, as in all other positions, you straighten up and throw overhand if you have the time. But many times a third baseman just does not have the time. It is a long way from third to first, and the runner is going away from you fast. It helps a great deal to know something about the speed of the runner and the speed of the man on base. You should also, when there is a man on first, keep that man in the corner of your eye, so you will know what sort of start he got. Then you will know, even as you charge in to pick up a bunt, whether you are likely to have a play at second base. That is one reason why I say the third baseman must be the fastest thinker. He has got to put all the facts together and come up with an answer in less than the time it takes to pick up the ball and throw it.

When there is a runner on second base who may advance on a bunt, then the third baseman has got still another fact to drop into his mental computer. Before the play, there will most likely be an understanding with the pitcher and catcher as to who will field the bunt. With a play coming up at third base, it is better if one of those players can field the ball, so you can break back to the base and be ready to kill off the lead runner—as you may very well do if the bunt is picked up quickly and cleanly. Of course, if the bunt is pushed right at you, with good speed, you will probably have to field it and hope the shortstop may get over there ahead of the runner.

Even if you do make the out at third, there may still be an out at first, or at second, if there were two men on. This possibility must be in your mind as you complete the play, so you can gun that ball to the place where you are most likely to make the next out. Yet in spite of the fact that the third baseman is very often concerned with getting rid of the ball in a hurry, he has to learn to stand his ground to make a tag play on a sliding runner. The place to await the throw on a tag play is astraddle the base, right at its middle. Just as at second, the baseman must hold his stance, ready to grab any kind of throw. Do not reach for the ball before it is thrown. Be relaxed and ready. Then, when you get the ball, put it right down against the base where the runner must slide into it. Hold it tight in both hands with your head over the play and the back of your gloved hand turned toward the runner. If the throw is really wild, you are going to have to abandon your post to get your body in front of the ball. But give it a chance to get to you. If you can get it without leaving the bag, by all means grab it and put the tag on quickly.

A runner on third base complicates a third baseman's life considerably, because there are always so many possibilities and options. You cannot let a man take too big a lead off third base. Yet you cannot afford to stick to the bag to hold him there—nor do you need to, for the threat of a steal is never so strong as it is at first base. All the same, you have to watch him to make sure he does not wander too far down the baseline before the pitch. If he gets farther away from the bag than you are, it is time to call for a throw to keep him closer. You may even have a pickoff signal with the pitcher to use when you have some speed boy on third, or some man who likes to take dangerous leads. It is very seldom a runner gets picked off third, unless he is really goofing off, but there is always the chance. And you should take care that you are not the one who goofs off. Don't let the pitcher forget there is a runner on third. Make sure he takes a look every so often.

Every runner likes to take a few quick strides toward home when the pitcher releases the pitch. As soon as the ball goes by the batter, if you are playing third base, you should hustle to the bag to give the catcher a chance to pick off the runner who has run down the line too far. His throw should come down inside the bag and you should be ready to tag the runner or trap him by chasing him down the baseline and snapping the ball to the catcher. But I want to repeat that here too you should not anticipate the throw's coming exactly where it should. Be astraddle the bag, knees bent, arms relaxed and out front, ready for *any* kind of throw.

If there is an outfield fly, with less than two out, and a runner on third, the chances are good that the runner will try to score. If the ball has gone to center or to right, you want to keep the whole play in view and be able to watch the runner. So your position should be *outside* the diamond. Hustle right off into foul territory. Keep one eye on the runner and one on the ball, and do not fail to remind the umpire to watch the runner's start. Point at the runner's feet and tell the umpire to make sure he does not start too soon. If he *does* start before the ball hits the outfielder's glove, be sure to make your beef right away. Otherwise the umpire may think that the man did not start too soon at all. If there is any doubt in the umpire's mind—and sometimes there is—you don't want to confirm the mistake by failing to protest at once.

If the ball goes to left field, you will have to move down the baseline to get a proper view of the proceedings, and it will be up to the shortstop to cover third. Seeing you down the baseline (you ought to go about halfway) the runner may even be tempted to fake a try for home on a short fly, just to draw a throw from the left fielder. If that happens, you are in the ideal spot to cut off the throw and bang it back to the shortstop to hang the runner up on the baseline.

If there is a man on first as well as on third, you have to remember that the man on first can also try to advance after a fly is caught. So even if you cannot make an out at home or at third, you may still cut off the throw and fire it quickly to second base (be sure someone is there to get it!) and put the other runner out. But you can't do that unless you are well down the baseline where you can keep track of all the action. You should also have made mental note, before the play started, of the possibility of an advance by the man on first base, so you can react with proper speed.

The man on third may also take off for home, not immediately after a fly has been caught, but after the man on first base has started for second base. If the throw then comes in to second, and a play is made there, the man on third is going to score. Do not ignore the tagged-up runner therefore just because he does not jump for home the instant the fly is caught. Let the relay man know at once what is going on and yell for a throw home.

37. About the toughest play the third baseman must make is the scoop and throw of the ball bunted just inside the baseline. The trick is to run *by* the ball, not straight at it, and pick it up with the bare hand as you reach it. You keep the knees and back bent and the eyes right on the ball. You often have to uncork your throw right from the fielding position, without straightening up.

◎

PLAYING THE OUTFIELD

There is a great deal to learn about playing the outfield but it is mostly specific stuff, such as how to play the walls in certain parks and how to adjust to the strengths and weaknesses of certain batters. Almost everyone who plays ball for any length of time can catch a ball on the fly, and everybody should catch a ball the way that is most natural to him. It is good if you can take a ball at shoulder height, because that speeds up your throw. And catching the ball high often gives you an extra chance at it if your first attempt misses. But is anyone going to tell me that Willie Mays, by catching a baseball hip-high, in that patented way of his, is doing things wrong?

No, you play the ball the way you are surest of it. And you learn to judge balls by catching a ton of them. An outfielder, if he hasn't already learned to do so, should practice running on his toes. Flat-footed running jolts your spine and makes your vision blur. And some of the best outfielders are always moving around so as to be able to take a ball on the run, moving toward the diamond. This gives a lot more momentum to the throw. But there is no way to learn to judge batted balls except by playing them. It takes a while to distinguish between the ball that is going to drop in front of you and the one that is hit well enough to carry over your head. When they come right at you, they look pretty much alike. In center field particularly, a line drive that seems to be headed right into your glove can suddenly take off as if it had turned on its rockets and keep right on going to the fence. But after a while you can tell by the sound of the bat striking the ball and by the speed with which the ball approaches whether the ball is going to poop out somewhere in front of you or is headed for the distant pastures.

Probably the most important thing an outfielder must learn is where to throw the ball after he catches or retrieves it. He won't know that unless he is awake all the time to where the runners are, how many outs have already been made, what the score is, and what sort of runners are on base. If he is catching a ball for the first out, with a man on second, he must understand that the chances are better than even that the runner, if he has any speed at all, and unless the fly has been caught fairly close to third, is going to try to get over where he can score on a sacrifice. So even before he closes his hand on the ball he must be preparing himself for the throw to third to hold the runner. If the runner is on third, and the caught fly does not make the final out, there is a fine chance the man will try for the plate. So the outfielder, unless he takes the ball hopelessly deep in the outfield, must look for the attempt to score. If the runner on third even bluffs a run home, the outfielder should fire that ball in. Bluffing a throw in a situation like that can give away a run to a smart baserunner.

Generally speaking, the throw is made ahead of the runner. That is, if an outfielder retrieves a ball hit safely on the ground in front of him, with the bases empty, the throw goes fast, hard, and low to second base. This throw is made to reach the fielder on a bounce, so as to avoid any overthrow that could give the hitter an extra base. An outfielder with a real strong and accurate arm, however, can sometimes catch a baserunner asleep by throwing *behind* him, as the runner makes a halfhearted turn for the next base. But this is the sort of play you make only when you have the utmost confidence in your throw and your ability to size up the action on the diamond. Ninety-nine times out of a hundred it is the wrong thing to do.

If there was a runner on first when the hit was made, the throw would probably go to third. But never make that throw automatically.

If you saw the runner get a good start, you should have told yourself ahead of time that he would probably try to go all the way and so you must get the ball in fast—either to the relay man or to the catcher.

A throw from the outfield to home plate has got to be low enough to be cut off in the infield. No one comes to a ball game to watch the outfielder make throws to the catcher on the fly, or to see how far he *can* throw. Your job is to get that ball back so it can put a man out, if not at home, then at some other base. So streak the ball in there about shoulder high. Don't snap it flat-footedly, like an infielder. Haul off and power it in with your full arm and back, and with a full stride. Sometimes you even need a hop and a stride. But make that long stride as you throw and don't throw with a short arm. Reach back and let it fly full strength.

Teamwork in the outfield is not so tightly organized as in the infield but it is still essential. There are no bases to cover out there, so every fielder can move freely into another fellow's territory to back him up, help on a relay, recover a dropped ball, or help round up a long hit. Sometimes a fielder with a bad arm needs someone handy to make his throws for him—as Mickey Mantle needed Tom Tresh one season when Mickey's shoulder was not up to the job of getting the ball in from center field. An outfielder should always figure that the next ball is coming to him and he should have his mind all made up as to what he will do with it—where to throw it if he catches it on the fly, where to throw it if he picks it up after it drops safely. When the ball does come out on the fly, the fielders must tell each other what they plan to do. The man who has the best angle on it—who can take it without looking into the sun, or who will be in the best position to throw when he gets it—should be the man to take the fly. Usually the center fielder has first call on everything. But no outfielder should just take for granted that the fellow next to him will know what is going to happen. If there is the slightest doubt as to which man can best handle it, the man who gets the quickest drop on it should yell "I got it!" and he should keep yelling until he is sure the other man has been called off. If you hear your teammate yell for the ball and you think you have a better chance for it, you can try to call him off. But if he persists and has a good jump on it, just take care to give him room. You can get close to him to be there if he misses the ball. But watch him and stay out of his way.

Wind, sun, and shadow can be hazards in the outfield. The wind is something you should check on from time to time, if it seems strong enough to move a ball out of the straight path. Toss up a little grass and see which way the wind is moving in your area. Sometimes it may be going in another direction from what it seems to be on top of the stands. If a fly stays up high enough, you can sometimes move into a position so that the wind will blow the ball toward you. Then it will be easier to handle than it would be if it were gradually moving out of your reach. And bear in mind that a high grandstand can sometimes create a wind current of its own, that will cause a ball to veer away from the stand and back into the playing field.

The sun can make a fielder look foolish if he gives into it too quickly. First of all, you must know exactly where the sun is and anticipate when a ball will go into it. Many times, you can look up at such a ball sideways, so as not to get the full glare of the sun straight into your eyes. And even if the first glance up blinds you (despite your sunglasses, which you must *never* be without), you can take another sidelong look and try to pick up the ball at an angle. It goes without saying that sunglasses must be flipped down *before* you look up toward the sun for the ball. In the late summer, or early fall, the sun can really become brutal, for it seems to look straight at you over the top of the stands. But you can't let it intimidate you. You should never throw up your hands in despair because you lose a ball in the sun. Stay with it! Try getting a different angle on it. You may get another look at it before it comes down, and you *may* have time to make a grab at it. Even if you have lost it completely, get your glove up there and be ready for it. It may even stick there.

An outfielder goes back after a fly ball in a somewhat different way from the way an infielder does. He can turn his back on it and watch it over his shoulder as he sprints along with it. Catching a ball this way is easier than it seems and requires mostly practice and confidence. The outfield is a nice smooth running surface, or it should be, and you need not spend time looking for baby carriages, used tires, and wagon tongues that you may trip over. You can fix your eye firmly on the ball and keep it there, never giving up until the ball settles down in your glove. Balls that seem out of reach can sometimes be caught up with by a real try. But if a ball is obviously going far beyond you there is nothing to do but turn and dig for the track (most ball parks, even in the minors, have a "warning track" that circles the outfield). If the ball is going to hit the fence you must be prepared for the rebound. That means that you cannot get too close to the ball, for it may bounce right through you if you don't have time to adjust to its sudden approach. It is good practice to have someone bang balls against the fence for you, so you can see what sort of course they follow and how far away you have to remain to be able to play them quickly. If you are deep enough so you have a chance to take the ball off the wall, then you should get back there and be ready to jump for it. Many a well-timed leap has taken a home run away from an enemy slugger.

Ground balls in the outfield should always be charged. Waiting for the ball to reach you is giving away extra bases. If it comes to you fast, however, you should get down on one knee and make sure you stop it. Don't try to be an infielder and take it in stride, unless it is falling very short. Of course, every good outfielder is bound to try shoestring catches from time to time. But remember they don't give out any extra points for breakneck tries in the outfield. A foolish effort to shoestring a ball that you just can't reach can turn a single into a triple. You must practice coming in on the short ones until you develop judgment as to just what you have a chance for and what you can't hope to get.

Some outfielders, even in the big leagues, occasionally forget that a runner on third can score after a foul has been caught. Now and then it is good tactics to let a foul ball go with a man on third, if catching it is going to mean getting too far away or too badly positioned to throw the man out at the plate. And of course with the winning run on third and less than two out in the last of the ninth, if you are in the outfield, catching a long fly is not going to affect the outcome at all. The man will still get home safely, whether the ball is caught or not. Better in those circumstances to get close enough to nail the short line drives and the bloopers that might otherwise drop safely in front of you.

Outfield practice during batting practice is better than getting fungoes. A ball batted off a pitch acts a whole lot different from those that come off a fungo bat. One of the advantages of the fungo hits is that the batter can put them where you need them, making you run right and left, come in close and back up to the fence. And if you can find some willing soul who will bat balls against the fence for you until you get tired chasing after them, you will really learn how the outfield ought to be played.

Center field probably requires the most skill, because the balls are harder to judge, and there is far more ground to cover. But it has the advantage of not requiring the sudden stops that often are necessary in right or left field, where the ball may bring you close to the stands. In a league park, center field can really offer problems because of the difficulty sometimes of picking up the ball as it darts up out of the background of the grandstand, through the mixed shadow and sunlight, and the tobacco-smoke haze. It is then that confidence and experience begin to count.

38. I was an outfielder almost all of my career. Everybody has his own best way of catching a fly ball. I used to like to take them high so I would have my arm in throwing position.

39. With the ball in my bare hand, I was ready to throw. And I tried always to *know* in advance where I would have to throw.

40. An outfielder does not have to snap the ball off flat-footed. As he throws he can stride toward the target and really get his back into the effort.

◎

HITTING

———

Everybody, even pitchers, will agree that hitting is the best part of the game. The cheers fans may give for a great pitching performance aren't in it with the noise they'll make at a succession of long blows by the home club. And I don't think there is anything in baseball that provides as much satisfaction to a player as laying good wood on a fast ball and sending it screaming out toward the fence. If ever they should divide baseball into offensive and defensive teams, I know a lot of ballplayers who would want to find some better way of making a living. I think some pitchers might quit if they could not get their licks.

The modern trend in batting is toward lighter, whippier bats. These are better for waiting on a pitch and lashing at it at the last moment, if it looks good. And they make for more long hits and lower averages, because you can't get hits off the handle too often. But youngsters still seem inclined to use bats that are too heavy for them. I am not sure that is altogether a mistake. It may very well be that using big brother's bat will not only make a kid feel more grown up but will help him develop the strength in hands, wrists, and arms that he needs. So while I would not want to see young players all coming to bat in a game with heavyweight wagon tongues, I think in practice an oversize bat may help.

Nearly every batting coach today will tell his charges that the important thing about a stance is to be comfortable. I sometimes wonder if we are not overdoing this comfort bit. In the last few years I have seen some hitters come up to the big league who get so comfortable at the plate that they go to sleep, or at least forget to swing. It is all right to be comfortable. But you should first of all make sure that you are getting into a position so you can do what you came up to the plate to do—hit a pitched ball into fair territory. The boys who step away from the pitch are "comfortable," all right. And so are the guys who fail to cock their wrists before swinging at the ball. But they don't often hit safely. And I think it could be proved that it is more comfortable to hold your arms close to your body as you bat. But it is a lousy way to bat.

I think where the idea of comfort comes in is in the actual position of the feet. Some men are built so they can hold their feet close together and take a big stride into the pitch when they swing. Then some of the lean, long-armed fellows do better if they take a spread stance and almost no stride at all, counting on shoulders and wrists to do all the work. So the position of your feet ought to be adjusted to your own knowledge of how you can get the most power into your swing, or how you can keep the best control of the bat. If you do not have the tremendous arm and wrist power that makes home run hitters, maybe you should keep your front foot more free and be ready to step into any sort of pitch and slap it into the nearest field—inside pitches into left for right-handers and outside pitches into right.

At any rate, you should not get so set on taking the stance that suits you that you are afraid to make adjustments to make your work more effective. Maybe you want to be a long-ball hitter and are not built that way. That was my trouble part of the time. I wanted to uppercut the ball into the bleachers when I was essentially a line drive hitter. So be ready to change your position at the plate until you find the one that combines comfort with effectiveness.

Another point that gets too little emphasis I think is the importance of a solid grip on the bat. A good strong grip is what you need to transfer the power of arms and shoulders through the bat into the ball. If your grip is not strong enough, the ball is going to shake the bat loose when contact is made and a good deal of the power will be lost. It will help your batting a great deal if you work hard on your grip. There are all sorts of devices to help you develop a strong grip. A rubber ball that you can carry around and keep squeezing when you have nothing else to do—or even when you are doing something else—

is about the simplest and is just as good as anything. Then when you take hold of the bat, don't be bashful about gripping it tight. If you watch some of the big hitters on my club, you'll see them work their hands on that bat as if they were trying to dig their fingers right into the wood, or squeeze the juice out of it. That makes for blisters in the spring and calluses in the summer. But it also means power when the bat meets the ball.

To enable yourself to meet a pitch quickly and efficiently, in any part of the strike zone, you have to keep your wrists and elbows away from your body. If you bring them in close, you'll be tied up in knots on a tight pitch and you won't be able to get a full free swing at any sort of pitch. Your arms must be free to swing that bat right through the ball and all the way around in a complete follow-through. So practice standing at the plate with the elbows up and away from the body.

The correct batting swing is a level one, with the wrists on the same level as the pitch, so that the whole length of the bat travels right through the area where the ball seems to be headed for. When you swing like that, the bat will seem to be cutting right at the pitcher's head—and some coaches used to tell us years ago to "knock the pitcher's head off," not for real, of course, but just creating that illusion as your bat blotted out your view of the pitcher's head when you took a practice cut. Actually, however, it is not always possible to keep the bat parallel to the ground with the wrists on a level with the ball. When the ball comes into the lower part of the strike zone, you could do that only if you dropped to your knees. So you have to drop the fat part of the bat a little on a low pitch. But you still swing the bat in a swift arc right around your body.

I have heard guys argue over whether you roll your wrists over when you meet the ball or after you meet it, or when. I think that kind of discussion is a waste of time. You can't take a batting swing apart and learn it a piece at a time. You have to learn it by swinging at a ball. And the very first thing you have to practice is what you learn in every other game that involves hitting a ball with any sort of stick or bat or club—keep your eye right on the ball. Your eye and your muscles will coordinate if you keep the target in view. It is only when you take your eye off the ball to spot the place where you think it may land that you start missing the ball by a foot.

So make your first batting practice, eye practice. Stand at the plate and watch that ball all the way, from the time the pitcher takes it in his hand until it reaches the catcher's glove. Try to see the stitches if you can. Then when you start swinging at the ball, see if you can see the ball hit the bat. Try to make out what part of the bat hits it. Get into the habit of sighting right down the bat every time you take a cut at the ball. It is the best habit you can develop.

Another habit you should develop is that of avoiding bad pitches. I know it grates you sometimes to stand and watch a lot of bad pitches go by. But if you make a habit of poking at those pitches, you are going to start doing that all the time and you'll have a hard time learning to let them go by in a ball game. Use those bad pitches to practice keeping your eye on the ball. Watch them go right by.

When you get a pitch that looks good to you, you should step right into it. Do not move your front foot away from the pitch or you will be falling away from it when you swing, and even if you connect you will hit it with only part of your power. Your step may be not much more than a shifting of the weight from your hind foot to your front foot. But it should be a forward movement. The swing itself, of course, begins with a backward motion, a tightening up to get the bat as far back as you can and still control it, and a general readying of the muscles to explode them at the ball. The real distance hitters, the Mickey Mantles and the Frank Robinsons and the Willie McCoveys, usually like to pile into every pitch with full power. That is all right if you have the strength to put balls consistently out of the park and if you have an eye good enough to lay off bad pitches. But most hitters do best to follow the advice Casey Stengel used to give us—to stroke the ball where it was pitched, without trying to pull it around to the nearest fence and without merely poking at it. As a matter of fact Casey used to *sing* this advice to us. Any time I was at the plate and took too fierce a cut at a ball and missed it, I could count on hearing that bullfrog baritone behind me. Well, actually it sounded rather more like a strangling crow, as Casey would chant: "Not too hard, not too easy, but tra-la-la!" Once you heard that, you had a hard time forgetting it.

Hitting the ball "where it is pitched" requires cutting down some-what on your swing, so you do not try to take hold of an outside ball and try to pull it over the nearest fence. Instead you drive it right back where it seems to be coming from. An outside pitch to a right-handed batter will reach the plate on the corner that points to right field, and if you meet it solidly there it should take off in the direction of right field. Your swing then will be curtailed so that, instead of turning you around in a complete follow-through, it will fade out just a little to your left. Naturally, a ball hit this way will not often go rocketing into the seats. But you may be surprised all the same at the distance you can get by just meeting the ball this way. If your swing is well-timed, and your grip is solid, you will meet the ball when all your weight is behind the effort—that is, when the ball is close enough to you so that you do not reach out, with your weight already shifted, to meet it. A change-of-pace pitch is designed to do just that to you— get you to commit yourself to the swing and shift your weight to the front foot, *before* the ball is near enough for you to meet it squarely. "Squarely" means when the bat is about at right angles to the path of the pitch. The best hitters learn to control the shift of their weight, so that they do not lean into the ball until the very last instant, and they can then check the swing if the ball suddenly dips out of the strike zone. It is not, however, quite so easy to check a swing with those whip-handled bats. They have a tendency to go right on through even when you are trying to stop them. But it can be done and it should be done if the pitch does not look right to you.

Many of the more slightly-built batters like to use thick-handled bats, because they count on getting hits off any part of the bat and they want to be sure to have wood enough to get the ball out of the infield. Some of the fellows will choke up just a bit to get better control of the bat. If you are not a professional strong-boy, or have not quite grown up to your frame yet, you may find that choking up on the bat—gripping it a few inches from the knob—will provide you with more confidence. And without confidence you cannot be a hitter anyway.

Where you stand in the batter's box may be related to your confidence too. This is chiefly a matter of style. But you should not stand away from the plate just because you are afraid you will be hit. If a pitcher can scare you back from the plate, he has you half-beaten. Some great hitters have stood far from the plate, but they have all stepped right into the pitch if it looked good to them. And they have all been able to handle a bat long enough to cover the entire width of the plate. Other batters have chosen to crowd the plate, so that any inside pitch that was not going to hit them would be in the strike zone. But what counts most is your attitude rather than your position. If you can convince yourself of your ability to hit anything that comes into the strike zone, then you will not flinch at an inside pitch and you will step right toward the pitcher to hit it.

My old teammate, Gene Woodling, crowded the plate about as close as anyone I ever saw, and I think because of this many pitchers assumed they could loosen him up with a tight pitch. But Gene would never give an inch and he was not the least bit backward about standing there and taking a strike just to see what the pitcher was going to try to get him out on. That's what you call confidence—to let the pitcher have a strike and never doubt that you can still find the pitch you want.

Gene always insists that the real contest is not between the batter and the pitcher but between the batter and the catcher. The catcher, says Gene, is the man who calls the pitches and sets the pitching pattern, so he is the guy you have to study and the guy you have to outguess— if you are going to guess at all. I don't believe you should go up to the plate with the idea of outguessing anyone. Rather you should be ready to wallop any pitch that looks good to you, without trying to anticipate whether it is going to be fast ball, curve, change-up, or slider. But there is no getting away from the fact that you are bound to do some studying over what the pitcher is likely to throw. Assuming that the catcher is the man who always decides what the pitch will be (and there have been pitchers, like Dean Chance and Ralph Terry, who insist on calling their own pitches), then it is good business to try to figure out what his pattern is. Some of them do get into a groove, and because the catcher shows up almost every day and you face the pitcher only a few times each year, learning what that groove is can be helpful. If you know when he is likely to call for the waste pitch and what he likes to call for when the batter is in a hole then you do have an advantage. Of course, you have to consider that the catcher is probably studying you too to find out what pitch you are likely to swing at and what you are especially looking for. So you may want to change your own pattern from time to time. You should always make a point in batting practice of working on the pitches they have been getting you out on. Some of the great hitters in history have crossed up the opposition by deliberately striking at and missing a pitch, so they could count on getting that pitch when men were on base and a hit would be more valuable.

There are some hitters who just don't want to know what pitch is coming. They find that "thinking" slows down their reactions at the plate and they would rather count on reacting automatically to what they see. But to most hitters it is a distinct advantage to know if they are going to get a ball they can tee off on or one that is going to fade down and away. So a study of pitching patterns, or a study of the patterns that catchers follow when calling the pitches, can pay off.

Keeping the eye on the ball is not really so easy as it sounds. Try doing it some time through a whole inning, as Casey used to ask the Yankees to do sometimes. Watch the ball around the diamond, watch it in the pitcher's hand. Watch as he rubs it up. Try to detect it when he is taking the sign. Watch it through the windup. That is what is meant by keeping your eye on the ball—not just picking it up as it approaches the plate. Really give it your full and devoted attention.

Our club spends an extra amount of time on bunting. Everybody practices bunting, but the pitchers work on it extra. Too many opportunities are blown and games are lost in the big leagues just because somebody takes bunting for granted. It is not really a simple art at all. It takes hard practice to learn to place a bunt properly. But a well-placed bunt can actually help bust a ball game wide open, as Jim Lonborg of the Red Sox demonstrated in the final game of the 1967 season.

It strikes me that the biggest fault with bunters is that they don't bend their knees enough. You simply cannot bunt a low pitch from a straight-up stance. Try it and you are almost certain to pop the ball in the air. The sacrifice bunt should be done from a squared-around stance, feet side by side, body facing the pitcher. You can hold the bat way up on the handle, with the hands close together, and just present the fat part of the bat to the ball. Or you can slide one hand up to the label on the bat, with the other hand on the handle, and offer the whole length of the wood. But you present it at near eye level, with elbows slightly bent, and knees flexed. If the pitch is low, you crouch a little so you can still get that ball at near eye level. You cannot hold the bat too tight or the ball will rebound too hard. So your grip is slightly relaxed, so the bat will give just a little to the pitch, and the ball will drop and roll gently away. You can control the direction of the ball by the angle of the bat. Aim the long surface toward the second-base line, and the ball will go out there. Aim it up the third-base line and you will send the ball in that direction. But don't stab at the ball. Often you can just catch it on the bat. Sometimes you may have to give it a light tap, as if you were hammering a tack—just a strong enough knock to get the ball past the pitcher— but that will be when you are bunting for a base hit. The sacrifice bunt just has to get on the ground in front of the plate, and roll away from the catcher.

Bunting practice is good for keeping the eye on the ball too, for you have nothing on your mind, when you sacrifice, except to get the bat on the path of the pitch, and it is natural to sight the ball carefully as it approaches. Make sure, however, that you wait for the ball. Do not push at it by straightening the arms. Keep the elbows bent and the grip relaxed, so that you will not pop the ball back to the pitcher. You do not try too hard to conceal your intent on this play, for of course everybody in the park knows when a sacrifice bunt is in order. As soon as the pitcher commits himself to the pitch, you bring your hind foot forward in the batter's box and face the pitcher squarely.

When you bunt to get on base, however, you do not bring that hind foot up until the ball is right upon you. A left-hander can drag a bunt right along in the direction of first base and get a good start on the fielder. But if you bat left-handed, remember that you do not start to run to first before you hit the ball. Actually, you move forward in the box, toward the pitcher. If you move away from the plate too soon you will not be able to cover the strike zone with your bat. So you bring your hind foot, your left foot, forward quickly as you slide your left hand up on the bat, to get better control. Your eye of course will be right on the ball all the while and you will deliver a light tap to the ball that will send it rolling to the right of the pitcher's mound. If you can get the ball by the pitcher—and it takes a little practice to learn just how to tap the ball to accomplish that— you are as good as safe, unless you are slow-footed, or unless the second baseman happens to have anticipated the play and is playing close to the baseline. If you are really slow afoot, you have no business trying to drag bunts. And if you catch the second baseman moving in toward the plate you should not pull this play either. But for a good runner it is a great weapon that can help demoralize the opposition and can also help build your own confidence.

When a right-handed batter bunts for a base hit, he does not drag it, of course. He pushes it. The move for him is to swing the bat down into bunting position when the ball approaches the plate. He too takes a step forward with his hind foot as he moves into the pitch. If you are a right-hander you can work this maneuver as a sort of interrupted swing, sliding the right hand up on the bat and bringing the left elbow in tight to the body as you step forward. It takes confidence, agility, and sharp eyes—and lots of practice—to master this. The ball can be tapped to either side of the pitcher's mound. But it probably works best when you find the third baseman playing well behind the baseline and can tap the ball in his direction.

A man who has good control of his bat can accomplish other things too, without trying to drive the ball out of the park. Casey used to beseech us all at one time or another to "butcher-boy" the ball, that is, chop down on it to send it bouncing through the infield. By choking the bat a little, you can put down an infield hopper that can really cause trouble. It is probably most effective when the third baseman is charging in to field an expected bunt and the shortstop is moving over to cover third. Then you can slide the hand back down out of the bunting position and fetch the ball a good sharp crack, to bounce it right through the shortstop's vacated spot. When this works right, there is not a fielder within hoping distance of the ball and you have yourself a good clean base hit, while the man on base can romp home.

Naturally, the pitcher is going to try to stop you from bunting, if he suspects a squeeze play. Or he will at least throw you pitches that are hard to bunt. Except on the suicide squeeze, however, the batter can wait and pick out the right pitch to bunt, because the runner is not supposed to go until he is sure the ball is on the ground. On the suicide squeeze, with the runner starting as the ball is delivered, the batter *must* get his bat on the ball, no matter what the pitch is like. Otherwise the runner is dead on the baseline. Managers usually expect pitchers, when a suicide squeeze is on, to throw the ball right at the batter. Under those circumstances it takes a pretty agile guy to keep from being hit and still get his bat on the ball. But that is your job—to protect that runner at all costs.

The hit-and-run play is not one that works too well in amateur ball, because there are not enough batters who can put a ball into right field on order. As a matter of fact, there have been major league managers who gave up on this play, or who made it just a steal with the batter hitting the pitch only if it was good. But this is a most effective play when it works and can move a runner into scoring position without costing an out. As I guess everybody knows, it is not really a hit-and-run but a run-and-hit, because the man on first base must start to run before the ball reaches the batter. It differs from a steal because the runner, instead of trying to outguess the pitcher and get a jump on him, waits until the ball is on its way to the plate before breaking for second. Then it is up to the batter to hit the ball behind the runner. If he hits ahead of him, the runner is going to run right into an out, for the shortstop will eat up the ball and flip it to second base. It may even be a double play, the very thing this maneuver was designed to prevent. But if the hit goes behind the runner, there is every chance that the second baseman will have moved toward second, leaving room for the ball to go right through. Or if it is hit safely to right field, the runner, moving away from the ball, will have an excellent chance of reaching third. And that is where you want him to be when this play is complete.

A right-handed batter can learn to hit almost any sort of pitch to right field—if the pitch is in the strike zone—just by delaying his swing a little and by cutting down on it, so that he does not pull the ball. An inside pitch is a pretty tough one to hit to right, and you are probably not going to put a home run in the right-field stands on such a pitch. But your job on the hit-and-run is merely to get the ball through the infield, behind the runner. If you swing late and meet the ball squarely, you will accomplish that. It is a skill worth a lot of practice, for it will make you a very valuable man at the plate, even if you don't rattle too many blows off the bleacher wall. As a matter of fact, if you do not have the arm and shoulder strength to hit for distance, you could do a lot worse than concentrate on learning bat control. The men who can hit the ball where they want it to go usually last a long, long time in baseball, for this is an ability that does not fade out so quickly as you get older.

Every batter at one time or another gets the feeling that he has lost his skills and is not going to get them back. But batting skill does not disappear overnight—as pitching skill sometimes does if a man injures his arm. The ability to get around fast on a pitch and put it out of the playing area does begin to fade eventually, as does speed afoot. But the ability to meet the ball with the bat lasts a man for many years. When a young hitter goes into a slump, it often means that the pitchers have discovered his weakness and are working on it. That is why it is vital that you know your own weakness and strive to overcome it. Make sure that your stance permits you to reach outside pitches and get the fat part of your bat on them. Make sure you are not off balance when you swing at any pitch in your strike zone. And make sure above all that you know your strike zone and do not suck after pitches that are well outside it. Take care not to overstride. If you get your weight forward too far or too soon, you are not going to get your strength into your swing. If curve balls give you trouble, ask for nothing but curves in batting practice and learn to wait for the ball before committing yourself to the swing. If inside pitches get you out, you may have to make a slight adjustment in your stance, so that you can get good wood on those.

But many batting slumps have psychological origins. Hitting requires intense concentration and supreme confidence. Anything that breaks your concentration or weakens your confidence may affect your ability to hit. Sometimes it is almost impossible to isolate the trouble. If a man is having trouble with his fielding, or is trying hard to learn a new position, and worrying about his ability to make the grade on that score, his hitting can fall off simply because his other troubles fill his mind so he cannot concentrate properly. That is why, when Andy Etchebarren was trying to turn himself into a big-league catcher for us, I told him to stick to his defensive work and that the job would be his even if his batting average fell off to .100. I know that it is impossible for a boy to learn all the manifold and complicated aspects of big-league catching and have much of anything left to devote to the job of hitting big-league pitching.

Concentration and confidence are closely allied. Lack of confidence can fill your mind so full of doubts and set you to thinking of so many different ways of curing your slump, that it will be impossible to concentrate on the baseball. And overconfidence, by which I mean that feeling that you don't really have to extend yourself to hit this pitcher, can cause you to take your eye off the ball, to lift your head to be ready to watch the ball fall into the stands, and to let pitches go by that you ought to swing at. The confident batter is the man who goes to the plate convinced that he has it in him to hit any pitcher who ever pitched, even if it takes an extra time to study what some particular pitcher is throwing. You get this confidence partly from accomplishment, and partly from the good solid feeling it gives you to have hold of a bat that feels just right and to be standing in a position that you *know* will permit you to swing good wood through any part of the strike zone. Lots and lots of hitting, and hitting practice will develop that confidence.

Concentration at bat has got to be fierce. You have got to get your eye on that ball and really hunger to hit it. Don't let it get out of your sight, unless the pitcher hides it. And if he does that you keep your eye on him until the ball shows up again. Then fix your whole mind on it as it comes to you. Count the stitches if you can. See exactly where it is coming. Watch it right to the bat or right to the catcher. There is no denying that this sort of concentration comes more easily to some men than it does to others. A guy who has a lot of projects in his head may find it hard to push them all out of his consciousness and just think about a small white ball and a wooden bat. As you make more money and take on more responsibility, there will be many thoughts begging for room in your mind and there may be days or even weeks when you cannot *really* get your mind clear enough to focus on hitting the ball.

A batting slump, therefore, may have a basis in something so far removed from the baseball diamond that it will never occur to you where to look for it. Just bear in mind that you cannot bring a single worry to bat with you. A slump will feed on itself sometimes just because the player will begin to worry about what may become of him if he does not start to hit again, or may spend his time at bat trying to think of what it might be that is getting in his way. So along with freedom from all worry and all other planning and daydreaming, you have to cultivate the faith that if you keep swinging you are bound to come out of your slump. If you begin to get overfussy about pitches, or spend all your time guessing with the pitcher or catcher, then you will fail to swing at a lot of good pitches. And you can't hit what you don't swing at.

If there really *are* mechanical difficulties, if you are without realizing it trying too hard for distance or lunging at the ball instead of waiting for it to come in range, then someone else can tell you about it. And you have to be ready to *listen*. Maybe that other guy cannot hit anywhere near as well as you can. Maybe he can't hit at all. But just because he stands outside you and watches, he may be able to see things you could never see. So don't be too proud to take advice or too wrapped up in your troubles to listen.

Once in a while a youngster starts feeling sorry for himself when he is in a slump, and then nothing can help him short of a good solid (but strictly psychological) boot in the tail. When you feel sorry for yourself, you are after sympathy and not criticism or even real help. You actually begin to enjoy your troubles in a way, until, without realizing it, you are actually digging a deeper hole for yourself and are imagining that someone, or everyone, has it in for you and is just making things worse for you on purpose. When a kid gets into that state, a manager can supply the imaginary boot in the tail by a good sharp bawling out. But sometimes the player has to supply the boot in the tail himself and go up to the plate full of determination to concentrate on nothing but pickling the next good pitch with the fat part of the bat. Or else he has to make up his mind to find exactly what he is doing wrong and to cure it by practice.

There is where the tremendous difference lies between what might be called "natural" hitters and real big-leaguers. The man with natural ability can go just so far, just as far really as the opposition will let him before they find out how to get him out. Then the game stops being just a pastime and becomes a profession. Then you can no longer swagger out there with an oversize bat and scare some kid pitcher off the mound. You are up against a crowd just as tough as you are and just as determined to get you out as you are to hit safely. You may learn within the first six weeks that you have a very serious batting weakness that the pitchers are all taking advantage of. So what do you do? Do you sit in the clubhouse and cry? Do you slam your bat on the ground or break it on the dugout rail? Do you write the home folks to send you the fare back to the farm, and go back to being a semi-pro? Or do you grit your teeth, tell yourself that no bunch of bush-league pitchers are going to make a monkey out of you, and come out for extra batting practice with the determination to learn to hit that pitch that you have been going out on, or to correct that habit that has been causing you to pop up, or to stop taking so many good pitches? Then baseball becomes hard work and requires a lot of inner drive to keep you going in the face of discouragement.

Many of the finest hitters have been sent back to the minors with puny batting averages and have had to fight their way back. Old Gene Woodling was batting about the same as his collar size when he was sent down to the Pacific Coast League and he had to alter his whole method of batting. Mickey Mantle struck out four times in four at-bats before he was sent down to Kansas City—where he went to bat twenty-three times and got *one* hit! Pete Runnels hit .356 with Chattanooga in the Southern League and then went six seasons in the majors before he reached .300 again. And he eventually won the American League batting championship.

So the ability to fight off discouragement, to come back out of slumps, and to plug along from day to day trying always to get a little better is just as important in major league baseball as natural talent. That may be one reason why they say that the hungry players are the best. They are the guys who know that if they don't make it in baseball they are not going to make a decent living anywhere else. So they just refuse to quit, they turn out for extra practice, and they work day and night to overcome whatever it is that is holding them back.

41. At bat, I favored a slightly closed stance and a rather short stride. I kept my elbows away from my body and the bat cocked, so I was actually hitting down on the ball.

42. The hitter should sight the ball right down the bat and try to swing the bat in a level arc.

43. A good follow-through is important. It helps you get your full strength into the swing. As you swing, the body weight shifts from the rear foot to the front foot.

44. A sacrifice bunt calls for offering the level bat to the pitch, with one or both hands moved up to give complete control. You bend the knees to get the bat on a level with the pitch and to get down where the bat is nearly at eye level.

45. When a right-handed batter bunts for a base hit, he does not move up in the box as for a sacrifice. Instead he tips the bat suddenly down, slides the right hand up toward the label, and "catches" the ball on the bat.

46. When a left-handed batter bunts for a base hit, he moves right up toward the pitcher. But he does not pull away from the plate until after the ball has met the bat.

◎

BASE RUNNING

———

Sometimes I think that great speed is what a baserunner needs least. Of course that is not true. But it does bug me often to see a real sprinter throw his speed away on the basepaths by trying to run too far and too often. There are one or two fellows around now who can really outsprint almost anyone else in the game but who just haven't got the judgment required to become good baserunners. They take needless chances. They don't know when to stop. And they have never studied on when to start.

You do need speed on the bases. A slowpoke team is one of the dullest sights in baseball. A man who is ready to break for second base on almost any pitch keeps the fans in an uproar, lifts the spirits of his mates, and helps demoralize the enemy. But more than speed, you need good judgment and a quick start. The baserunner, as everyone must know by now, steals on the pitcher. He has to study pitchers closely to detect the little giveaway move that will tell when the pitcher is *really* going to throw to the plate. If he waits until the ball is on the way to the plate, he has little chance of reaching second base safely, so he has to start while the pitcher still has hold of the ball.

This means taking a chance. Every attempted steal is a gamble, because there are times when the pitcher's "move" will fool you and he will fire the ball over to the first baseman and catch you on the baselines. So if you are a man who has to have a sure-thing bet every time, then you'll never be a base stealer. But you can be a reasonably good baserunner, if you'll use your head as well as your feet.

You become a baserunner as soon as you hit a ball into fair territory. You should not wait around, however, to help the umpire decide if a ball is fair or foul. You should dig for first as soon as the ball leaves the bat and go for it full tilt until and unless the umpire calls you off. Sometimes, of course, a ball is obviously foul the moment you hit it, and you do not run on those. But if that ball goes out in front of you and seems to be headed for fair territory, or near it, you should take off for the base. Fans, and managers, want to see a ballplayer run out every possible hit. Believe me, no one likes a ballplayer who will surrender on a ground ball—unless he is so obviously crippled that he would be risking serious injury.

One of the easiest and best ways to make a good impression on your manager when you break into baseball is to *run*. There was a rookie a few years ago who even sprinted to first base on a base on balls, and he had the whole league talking about his hustle. You don't need to do this, but the least you can do is try to turn every ground ball into a hit by running. Even the easy rollers back to the pitching mound sometimes take funny spins and turns. Occasionally a pitcher falls down trying to field the ball or just fails to pick it. Once in a while an easy grounder will stick in the webbing of a fielder's glove. Even soft pop flies have been known to fall safe, with the runner, going all out, ending up on second base. So the first thing you ought to practice as a baserunner is getting a fast start for first and running full speed on everything that might be fair. When one of those one-in-a-million accidents happens, you want to be right there to take advantage.

When you run to first, you run outside the baseline. If you run right on it, or inside, you may find yourself called out for interfering with the throw. If the ball went into the infield you concentrate on making first. You'll make it quickest if you hotfoot it right along in your regular stride. Don't ever get the idea that the final step should be a gazelle-like leap or a slide, for if you break your stride with something like that, you'll actually lose a split second. As you don't need to hold to the base when you get there, you can barrel right along with all the power you own and let your momentum carry you where it will.

If the ball you hit went into the outfield and you have reason to hope for more than one base, you start to make your turn for second before you get to first. Incidentally, while you were at bat, or even better, while you were in the on-deck circle, you should have looked over the position of the outfielders, so you could decide what sort of throwing arms you were up against and where a ball would have to land to give you a chance for extra bases. Then as you approach first you can swing out in an arc that will permit you to tag the inside of the base and then head *straight* to second. Even in baseball the shortest distance between two points is still a straight line. A swing through the outfield just adds to your chances of being put out at second.

One of the many things that used to try the patience of Casey Stengel was to see a seasoned ballplayer run from first to second with his eyes on the ground. I have heard him explain at least half a hundred times that there are no deep holes on big-league baselines, and so a base-runner can afford to look to see what is happening to the ball. If the ball is mishandled in the outfield, or has bounced through to the fence, you may have a chance for still another base, and you should start for third *before* you reach second. Once more you swing out in a short arc that permits you to tag the inside corner of second base. Then you dig straight down the line for third base. If the ball is behind you, you will have to count on the coach to tell you what to do as you approach third—to slide, to make a turn, to tag the base, and dig for home. But if you can see the ball, then you must make up your own mind. Waiting for a sign from the coach might cost you half a step, which you may need. Of course you must watch the coach, particularly if there is a runner ahead of you. But if you can see the ball, the coach is going to expect you to decide for yourself what you are capable of.

If you stop at first, you have the problem of avoiding a pickoff, reading the signs the third-base coach or the batter may give for hit-and-run, steal, or bunt. If you know your business well, and can get a fast start, the manager is probably going to let you make up your own mind about when to steal, or else just give you a general directive you can apply on your own. But the other signs you should understand and should watch for. You should have gone over them in your mind even before you came to bat.

Generally speaking, the proper lead to take at first base is the length of your own body plus one step. That is, you can beat the pickoff throw back to the base at any time, with a step and a dive. But the real base thieves will take just as much as they can get, and some of them, like Luis Aparicio, will just stroll off toward second base until the pitcher notices them. This "walking start" is not for everyone, however. I think a good wide stance and slight crouch, with the weight just a little more on the right foot than the left, will give you a proper jump. Which foot you move first is a matter of taste. A lot of runners find it more natural to move the left foot first, and start with a crossover step, even though the geometry demons used to advise taking the first step with the right foot, it being the one closer to where you wanted to go.

Here again, the criterion is your own "comfort" or natural inclination. If you find it more natural to start with a crossover step, then that is what you should do. Trying to learn a new way to do it would slow you down and might even leave you tangled in your own feet. I'd be willing to bet that half the leading base stealers in the business could not even tell you offhand which foot they move first. They'd have to get into position and try it to make sure. But once you make your start, you have to give the effort all the power your legs possess. You can't be halfhearted about stealing base. You have to explode into your top speed and barrel into that base like a projectile.

Every baserunner has to know how to slide. It is really easy to learn, for it is just falling down on purpose and it comes natural to you if you develop confidence. Actually it's fun, if you can find a nice soft surface to practice on. I've seen kids practicing in mud, splashing the stuff all over themselves and shooting along like a surfboard. But any good slippery surface will do. If you can practice in your stocking feet, you'll lessen the risk of getting your spikes caught. Once you get the hang of keeping the soles of your feet turned slightly upward so the spikes are off the ground, you will not be in any danger.

But even big league sliders often forget to get their hands in the air, and because of that they sometimes jam a finger and put themselves out of action. The traditional way of reminding yourself to get your hands up and off the ground is to grab up two handfuls of loose dirt as soon as you take your position off first base. Somehow it is just human nature to hold the hands high when you have something in them. You can pretend you're bringing home a couple of sandwiches if you want and are trying to get them there in shape to eat.

The men who are looking for the extra base always use the straight, pull-up-type slide. This is the one where you extend one foot and bend the other leg at the knee so that you slide along on your shinbone. This position enables you to come promptly to your feet once you hit the base, so you can be ready to keep going if the throw has been bad or the baseman has booted the ball. Many slides, however, are for the purpose of avoiding a tag and so the runner will aim his front foot, and his body, away from the base, sliding along on hip and thigh, with the other leg bent outward, so that the foot can hook the base, without offering too much body to be tagged. To do this properly you have to watch the fielder as you approach, and slide on the side opposite from where he stands. You have to be able to slide with either leg extended and the weight on either hip. But you have to be careful to keep your hands up. And you have to avoid turning your body to one side or the other. If you turn your body, you are bound to get your hand on the ground and you have a fine chance of jamming a finger or thumb. What you do really is sit down suddenly and ride in on your tail, with one leg out to hook the bag in passing.

You never catch anyone writing this down in a book, but the fact is that some sliding is for the purpose of taking the pivot man out of the play, when a double play is in the making. A big leaguer who will not make an effort to break up a double play is just not going to stay long in the big leagues. This is an aggressive aspect of the game that many school coaches will play down. Maybe they should, because it seems to belong more to football than baseball. And there is no questioning the fact that it is a form of interference with a fielder. But it is legal interference because you do have a right to slide, you have a right to the baseline and room on the base, and no umpire is going to try to worry out the difference between an honest effort to beat the tag and a deliberate effort to prevent the relay. So when there is a runner who is likely to be out at first behind you, you should not simply surrender when you see the throw has beaten you. Slide straight in, with the aim of carrying right over the base, or right through the baseman. Of course, you are not going to chase him if he has completed the putout and has retreated off the baseline. But if he is anywhere where you have a right to be, you must exert that right, without hesitation or squeamishness. Any professional ballplayer who plays pivot man on a double play knows he is fair game for a takeout slide and he is not going to resent it. He is going to try hard to avoid it, of course, but that's what you want him to do.

You just don't want to let him stand there and take careful aim for first base. To do that is a form of surrender on your part. And a baserunner should never surrender.

You especially should not surrender when there is another runner on base. If you should find that a throw has beaten you to second, when there is a man on third, then you should keep dodging and bluffing back and forth just as long as you can in the hope that the other man can score. Or if you are caught between third and home, with a runner on first, you should stay alive long enough for the other man to reach second base.

A runner on second is still in danger of a pickoff. His danger is increased by the fact that the pitcher is allowed to bluff a throw to second, and so you cannot ever be sure what he is going to do next. But if you remind yourself that there has to be a man at the base to tag you out, you can take care not to allow a fielder to get closer to the base than you are—or to get close enough to beat you to the base if you both start together. You are in a position to watch the second baseman, and the coach at third base will keep telling you whether you are safe from the shortstop. Of course, you will use your own eyes and ears too, and not get so interested in the action elsewhere that you forget what is going on around you.

As on every base, the runner at second takes a few fast steps toward the next base as soon as the ball is on the way to the plate. But unless you are a fast man, you will not get any special advantage from a long lead off second. Instead, you may lay yourself open to a quick snap throw from the catcher when you are too far off to get back. A short lead is best for the average ballplayer here, as long as he remembers to move along a few steps when he sees the ball on the way to the batter. It should go without saying that you keep your foot on the base until the pitcher is on the mound. He is not allowed to take a stance there without the ball in his possession, so if he is slow about getting up there, it may mean that someone close by has got the ball hidden in his glove. You stay put until the pitcher is up around the rubber. Then take a short lead. Be sure to look at the coach for any sign he may have. And be sure to see where the fielders are playing—outfielders as well as infielders. You don't want to have to stop and gawk around after a ball is hit to see if anyone is in a position to field it.

If the ball is hit ahead of you when you are on second base, and there is no runner on first to force you, you do not try for third until you are sure the ball is going through. If the ball is fielded in front of you, you had better hang on to what you've got. There may be instances when a hard ground ball will pull a fielder far out of position and even leave third base uncovered. If that happens you will have to use your own judgment about trying to reach third. The coach can't tell you what to do. You know your own pace best and know what sort of start you have got. If you have moved up with the pitch and have a little momentum, and if you have good speed, then you may be able to help yourself to the base.

If the ball is hit to the right side, and you have remembered to move up properly with the pitch, then you have every chance in the world of making it safely to third base. If the ball was bunted and fielded quickly, however, your chances are slim. And you don't take wild chances on the baselines.

You take a chance and run only when there is something to gain. If there is one out when you are on second and the play is going to make it two out, it is still going to take a hit to score you so you might almost as well be on second as on third. (Unless you have second sight and can see a wild pitch coming soon.) But if the play is going to make the first out, it is worth taking a chance to be on third with one out. In that situation an out can score you. Try not to make out number one in trying for third base, however. Do not stretch your hit beyond second with nobody out unless you are confident you can make it. And you should determine that *before* you get to second and before the coach beckons you on. Of course, if the ball is misplayed in the outfield, you may have an extra base right there for the taking. All the more reason for looking out there to see what is happening to the ball. Remember, as Casey used to say again and again, there are no holes in the baseline for you to fall into.

A runner can often advance from second to third on a long fly, particularly a fly to right field. If the ball is hit in the air, take off for third and stop about halfway to check what is happening. If the fly is a long one that is going to be caught, your move is to scamper back to second base to be ready to break for third as soon as the ball touches the fielder. If there is anything doubtful about the length of the fly, remember what I just said about taking chances. If it is out number one, it's worth a chance. Otherwise, no. If the ball is hit safely, you have to decide right away whether you are going to have a chance to score, because you have got to swing out before you get to third so you can cut straight for the plate. The coach will be part way down the line to throw the stop sign if the ball is coming back unusually fast. But unless he is down there to flag you down, pour on all the juice and let the on-deck batter signal you as to whether to slide or come in straight up. If you hesitate at third base and wait for a sign to move ahead, you have lost several strides and will not make it home anyway unless there have been some misplays in the field. Of course, you once more have to use your head to decide whether to take a chance or not. If you are the tying or winning run, then you have something worth taking chances for. If you see the throw come into second base, you should round third and take a few strides toward home—not so far that you can be picked off with a fast throw, but far enough to get a good start if the throw gets away from the base-man. If it does, and you have taken those extra few strides, you have a good chance to bring in the run.

A runner on third base has got to be particularly alive, for there are many things he can do to help the cause. He can bluff a dash for home, he can score on the front end of a double steal, he can score on a sacrifice fly, he can score on a bunt, he can score on a caught foul fly, he can score on a passed ball or wild pitch, he can scurry home on an infield roller, or score after a dropped throw. But he can also be picked off the base if he dopes off. Catchers love to nail napping runners on the third-base line.

To score after a sacrifice fly, you have to keep your eye on the ball. You must have a foot in contact with the base until the ball touches the fielder. But that does not mean you cannot *move* before the ball touches him. As long as you do not take your foot off the base until after the ball reaches the fielder, you can move all you like. What Frank Crosetti taught me was to stand with one foot on the base. Then you could stride forward with your other foot just *before* the catch, and your foot that was on the base would come off the base the instant the fly was caught. In this way you could get a moving start and still not break the rule.

It is not the coach's job to start you on a play like this. You have to keep your own eye on the ball and time your own start, because there is a split second always between seeing the ball caught and taking the step. But if you put in an added split second, between the time the coach says "go" and you go, you may be giving up enough time so they can put you out.

On third base, there is only one man, as on first, who can take a throw to pick you off. (I am not talking about trick plays where one player may run in as if to get a bunt and another may sneak behind you.) So all you have to do is take care not to take so big a lead that you cannot beat the third baseman back to the bag. The farther off he plays the longer lead you can take. And again you "move up"— moving sideways if you like—when the pitcher lets the ball go toward the plate. In leading off third base, you should always move in *foul* territory, off the baseline, so there will be no danger of your being clipped by a hot ground ball and counted a putout. In returning to the base, when the catcher has the ball, always move right on the baseline. In this way you will make it more difficult for the catcher to get a fast throw off to the baseman.

A ground ball, even if it is fielded in the infield, may still score you from third, provided the fielders are not playing in close to cut off the run. If you take care to move up with the pitch, you should have a good start, and if the ball is not hit too sharply you can keep right on going. Even if you have no real chance to score, a good bluff can force a throw home and avoid an out at first. But a bluff must not be reckless. That is, you should be *really* bluffing and should not get past the point of no return. A good quick start, with lots of leg action, and without any hesitation, may jump an infielder into firing the ball home.

You can make a try for home on a short fly too if there is another man on base, in the hope of advancing him from first to second, even if you get caught. If the throw does beat you, you should keep dodging back and forth until the other runner is at second.

A steal of home is something you can usually pull only when the pitcher gets careless. But if you keep a close eye on him, the time may come when he forgets to check your lead and you can really get a blazing start. You have to be *fast* for this, for there is very little time to get there. A strong slide will give the catcher very little to tag and may even cause him to drop the ball, because he will have to grab it and lunge for you in the same move.

When the bases are full, most pitchers will go for the full windup, with a forceout at every base. When this happens, you have a chance to get a good moving start, walking or shuffling down the line, with your eye on the pitcher, and starting to move fast when he lets the ball go. Again you have to take care not to go beyond the point of no return. But if the ball is hit, you have an excellent chance of scoring.

Even with a drawn-in infield, it may be possible to score on a ground ball—a well-placed bunt or one of those "butcher-boy" choppers that bounce high and seem to waste a lot of time coming down. So you stay alert even when the odds are against your scoring. And you keep looking for the break that will let you go in. Never stop watching the ball and never take for granted that the catcher is going to hang onto the pitch. Even the best of pitchers throws a wild one occasionally. And even the best of catchers sometimes lets a ball go through.

If you are on the front end of a double steal, with the man on first trying for second, you let him go first and you do not start until the catcher has the ball and prepares to throw it. This is a gambling play and you must be prepared to gamble against the catcher's bluffing. Just as soon as he pulls that ball back to throw it, you have to take your life in your hands and start full tilt for the plate. Maybe you will lose the gamble and the catcher will snap the ball down to third base, catching you in a rundown. Well, now you know the man is safe at second and you do your best to keep the play alive. If the catcher has the ball, you bluff hard toward him, then run away. If the third baseman, or someone on that side of you, has the ball, you bluff hard toward him and run the other way and you keep this up just as long as you can. Someone may still drop the ball, or get a bad throw that allows you to get safely by him. And if you keep it going long enough, then the runner may make it all the way to third. (Incidentally, if you should ever get to third base and find another runner there ahead of you, remember it is *his* base and you can be tagged out even if you are standing on third.)

When you slide in to score it goes without saying that you try to avoid the tag. That is, you slide *away* from the catcher, and drag your trailing foot over the plate. But if he is standing astraddle the plate, then the slide should be straight in, pull-up style, with the front foot going between the catcher's feet. That's the quickest way of getting there.

One of the worst things a baserunner can do in my book is get himself doubled up on a line drive or a bunt. There is just no excuse for this, unless there is a play on that has forced you to advance regardless, or unless the bases are full and you are forced out. If you are on first or second, and the sacrifice bunt is on, it is up to you to make sure that the ball is not popped up. Do not run blindly for second. Turn and make sure the ball is on the ground. Even on the hit-and-run play there is no excuse for your getting doubled. There is nothing to keep you from glancing back at the plate even as you are flying to second. If the ball has been hit in the air, hold up until you are sure it is going to hit the ground safely. When there is no special play on, all the more reason for your watching the ball after it leaves the bat. The baseline coaches will give you signals, of course, to tell you if you can advance or should stop. But you should not leave to them the job of telling you if a ball has been caught or is on the ground. Line drives especially should be watched to make sure an infielder does not snag them on their way through.

Let me repeat what I said about knowing the tactical situation— whether you represent the tying or winning run, whether your club needs a hatful of runs or only a couple, and how many men have made out already. These facts will all influence your decisions on the baselines. If a short fly makes the first out, then you probably will not risk trying to score from third. There is a chance of another longer fly, even of an infield roller, that can bring you in. But if the fly makes the second out, it is going to be your last chance to score on an out and, if the run is vital, you may want to take a chance. The gamble is worth it. And you should always give a good bluff on a short fly to the outfield anyway. Sometimes you can get the outfielder to bluff a throw, which will cost him time, and this may be all you need to come in on.

If there is a runner ahead of you, naturally you have got to be aware of him. When you move from second to third, you have to watch the third-base coach to make sure he has sent the lead man on in. If there is a runner on first when you are on third, you must look for a play at second on a fly ball. Maybe the throw will be mishandled. If you are moving from second to third on a hit, perhaps there will be a throw to second base. Give a look as you round third and see if perhaps the ball has got loose.

Don't let your speed carry you past the base where you belong. You may have to slide to the base to keep from overrunning it. But if you start to slide, never try to stop the slide in the middle. More ankles and legs are twisted that way than in a full slide. Once the slide has begun, give yourself to it, and come to your feet quickly if you think there is a chance for another base.

While a runner should have his speed under control, that does not mean he should jog along on the baselines. I like to see a man get where he is going *fast*. Maybe you can see that the play is not going to get you past second. But don't concede that. Get down there at top speed and be ready, in case something behind you goes wrong for the opposition. Just don't get so speed happy that you get halfway past every base before you check to see what is happening. That is not baseball. That's just showboating.

Not that showboating is always to be deplored. A fast man ought to try to keep the pitcher uneasy. He can do that by taking just a bit more than a regular lead off the base, by bluffing a steal on every pitch, by making bluff moves toward second to make the pitcher throw. The more the pitcher thinks about you when you are on base, the less brain power he has to spare for the batter. And a moving object in the range of the pitcher's vision is far more distracting than a stationary one. The umpire is not going to let you wave your hands or your torn shirt-tail to unnerve the pitcher. But little scuffling false starts and body movements are fine—if you can get away with them. If you are not fast off the mark and more than ordinarily agile, don't try them.

Remember, too, that every throw means a possible error, so draw throws when you can, particularly as you round third. You do not need to go so far as not to be able to jump right back. But you can round the base—if the ball is across the diamond—and force them to throw to make you come back.

In short, you should be *thinking* all the time you are on base. Look for opportunities to move up. Watch the coaches for signs. *Know* where the ball is. Know where the fielders are. Know what your own speed is capable of. Know what other runners are on base. Know what the score is. Know what the count is on the batter and how many are out. Know if you will be a forceout at the next base or will have to be tagged. Know what has happened to the runner ahead of you. Don't wander off the base before the pitcher goes to the mound. Do not get up to brush off dirt until you have asked for time. Stay in the ball game. Do not become a spectator.

47. Here is the way big Boog Powell attempts to break up a double play. He is not trying to do anyone an injury, just to keep the infielder from getting set to throw.

48. Making a tag one-handed is a chancy business when the runner is sliding into the base.

49. Sometimes the impact of the runner's body will knock you right loose from the ball and the runner will be safe.

50. This is the right way to use the pull-up slide. You get *both* hands high in the air and slide straight in on the bent leg. Do not roll your body to the side or you may get one hand down and injure a finger.

51. The catcher can wait for the throw in front of the plate and leave a good portion of the plate open for the runner to aim at.

52. But once the catcher has the ball in his hand, he can step right in front of the runner and make him slide into a tag.

WINNING BALL GAMES

I have played for winners and played for losers and have managed both, so I think at this point in my life I can begin to figure out what makes the difference between the two. In baseball I think the number one secret ingredient is playing for the club—playing to win, sticking together, working to help bring in those runs, even if you don't get them in your personal record. I tell my pitchers that I don't care at all about those CG's (complete games). It's the W's (wins) that matter. And if the W goes to some guy who has to come in and help put out the fire for a few innings, it doesn't make any difference. The big thing is *we* win.

As I have already said, that's why I like a big, active bullpen and that's why I am so much quicker to change pitchers than some other managers may be. My guys are all conditioned to sacrificing their own records for the good of the club. I don't mean they all like it. Some of them still growl and sputter about being lifted when they feel sure they can get the next guy out. But they don't hold any grudge and they don't hate me for it.

And the rest of the club is adjusted to the idea too that I may ask even the best of them to sacrifice a time at bat for the sake of putting a run on third. Maybe some of our strong boys get a little irritated when they have to hit to right instead of going for the bomb. But they don't hate me for that either.

Not that I would care too much if they hated me as long as they respect me. For that is another quality I think a winning club must have

—respect for the leader, even if they hate his guts. They used to say about McGraw that some of his men would daydream about pounding him over the head with a bat. But there never was an old-time Giant who did not respect McGraw.

We respected our boss on the Yankees too. Believe me, I used to be ready to explode sometimes when I would be benched because a right-hander was pitching. But I had learned that that old man knew what he was up to, that even when he looked as if he was half asleep on the bench, he would come wide awake if anybody made a mistake—and he would recite chapter and verse. Stengel used to joke with the players at times and he was on friendly terms with most of them. Just the same, he did not believe in socializing with them. When they were out of town, there was only one man who could sit and drink beer at the bar of the team hotel—that was Casey. The players had to go somewhere else to do their relaxing.

Keeping the players at arm's length this way, in their off hours, is good for everybody. It relieves the players of constraint and it keeps any player or group of players from getting palsy with the boss to the point of disrespect. When I am sipping a beer somewhere during the season and one of the players comes in, I may ask him to lift one glass with me. If he refuses, I don't press him. And if he does have one, I expect him to take off immediately afterward.

I think the manager can contribute most to keeping a team winning by keeping them happy—by encouraging them when they are down, by praising them when they are going good, and by working to keep alive that one-for-all, all-for-one spirit. If you have a bunch of big leaguers working for you, you are not going to have to burden them with too many instructions. But you can keep them on their toes, make sure they stay in top condition, keep sore spots from developing, and help them enjoy their victories. Boy, when a club is winning, there is no better place to be than on that bench or in that clubhouse. But sometimes it takes a little petting and coaxing to keep a club loose when they have dropped four or five in a row. And keeping them loose in those times is the manager's job.

As I said, I don't believe in a lot of meetings. And I don't turn the clubhouse into a holy of holies where we cook up secret plans to win the next ball game. Just the same, we do have rules and I like to see them obeyed. Having been over the ropes myself I think I know every scheme a ballplayer ever invented for beating the curfew or grabbing a little extra goof-off time, so not many fellows fool me twice. I want the players to get their rest, to be in condition to play baseball, and to keep their minds on baseball as long as they are in the park. There are no red-hot card games in our clubhouse. And the only telephone is right on my desk. I have known of managers who took their players to the races, who talked racing to them day and night, who allowed the players to sit around before a ball game and make race-track selections. But if a man in my clubhouse tries to open a discussion of horse racing or dog racing, he'd better be kidding. And we operate in a city where horse racing gets right into your blood.

But even in enforcing these rules, I like to treat the guys the way I would have wanted to be treated when I was a player. I know how it galled me to have anyone bawl me out in front of my teammates, or to treat me as if I were a high school kid. So as I explained earlier, I take extra care to avoid that. This is important in developing that loyalty that you have to have to get fellows into the mood to make sacrifices for the good of the club. If you don't put a guy down in front of his mates, and if you treat him like an adult, as good as the next guy, he is going to respond—maybe not by doing exactly what you suggest, but at least by respecting you and being willing to follow orders in a ball game.

Of course, treating the players the way I would want to be treated does not say it all because I was a very different breed of cat from some of the guys we have with us. Maybe what I should say is that I try to adjust my treatment to the nature of the guy I'm dealing with. Some guys don't need any special handling, and I can talk straight out to them and not be afraid of leaving a sore spot. Other players have to be gentled a little more. One or two are pretty moody, inclined to get down on themselves, and you can't find fault with them unless you mix in a little praise. At least one guy is like a big kid, finding it hard to get really serious about any matter. You have to needle him a little and even get a little sore at him or he won't even believe you. Above all you have to talk ballplayer language to this crowd. By that I mean you have to use words that are plain, and even a little profane or the ballplayer just won't be with you. It's all right for the general manager to go school-teacherish with the players when they talk contract. But when you want a guy to stop swinging at pitches out of the strike zone, you've got to underline your point and make it in the kind of language that men use in the clubhouse.

I think most ballplayers are good fellows to deal with, if you take the trouble to think of them as individuals and don't try to bully them or let them bully you. They are different from show business types, even though they are in the entertainment business. You may run into temperament, especially with the pitchers, who have a lot more on their minds than the other players, and who have to be more individualistic, by the nature of the game. But you never seem to find any real phonies, or any guys so overwhelmed with their own importance that they have to be babied and catered to and flattered. Those types just can't last in a game where a man becomes a star by becoming an effective member of a team. So with a few exceptions ballplayers are good to have around, pleasant to deal with, and easy to talk to.

You have to understand that the picture you get of a ballplayer through the press is not always what the man looks like to his manager or his mates. Some ballplayers just cannot be themselves with writers. They resent intrusions into their private affairs. Or they may have some resentment they dare not express against the manager or the club or even against themselves, and let it explode instead against a writer, with the result that they create a bad "image." Or they may look like fair game to some writers, who think they are doing the player a favor by putting funny remarks in his mouth and making him the hero of anecdotes that never took place. Or some writer himself may have a private beef that he works out by making much out of some minor episode in a player's career, with the result that there is constant irritation.

But the manager has to know the player the way a father knows his kids. Not that he should treat them like kids, but he should at least understand them. He cannot afford to have likes or dislikes. They are all his club and it is his job to get along with them and to keep them getting along smoothly with themselves. Maybe some guy does pop off a lot. If he wins ball games, he can pop off day and night. Maybe some guy forgets to hand out a cheerful hello or growls at being taken out of the lineup. You can't hate him for it, as long as he is holding up his end during the ball game.

I make an effort to get along with the ballplayers at all times, overlooking their bad moods as they overlook mine. I'm not afraid to sit and gab with them when we are away from the clubhouse. I'll play cards in the hotel room, or exchange funny stories. But once we get to the park, I want them to recognize that I am the manager and that I am running the ball club. I find that if a player respects you, and knows that you appreciate his skills and will not put him down in public, you can talk to him a lot more plainly than you could otherwise. They don't resent my "What the hell goes on here?" or even my strong language offered to them in private conversations. They know I am on their side, and that both of us have the same goal—to win the ball game.

Of course, losing ball games is poison to even the sweetest of natures and can cause more dissension in a club than a stolen girl friend. When nothing you try seems to work, when you drop games you know you ought to win, and when you keep on dropping them in spite of everything—then men begin to snarl at each other, begin to look for somebody to blame it on, and begin to gather into cliques to mull over all their gripes. As it happens, I have never really been through a real siege of that and until I do I suppose I will not rate as an "experienced" manager. But as a ballplayer I have lived through such times and I know for one thing how little the manager can do to stop the downhill slide.

The ironic part of that is that the manager is eventually the man who will take the rap for the "dissension" and the "collapse." Yet all he can really do is try to help the fellows stay loose, to forget the last game and still go out and give their best to the next one. With young players, that is sometimes not so easy as it sounds. You may have to take one aside and really lay into him, to get him to stop feeling sorry for himself. And you sometimes have to get your coaches to break up the cliques. The coaches are closer to the players and can mix with them more intimately than the manager. They can also tip a guy off, confidentially, that he is getting in wrong with the skipper and should straighten out.

It is one of my theories that, while a team should stay loose, it should not be allowed to take its losses with too light a heart. I always liked the story of the old-time pro football player in Canton, Ohio who would not let his teammates sing on the train home from Massillon after a defeat. I won't stand for any card-playing on the bus after we lose, or any horseplay or hilarity. The guys can go out and relax as they please after we get to the hotel, as long as they don't miss curfew and as long as they show up at the park ready to play. If a guy is not in shape, I'll run him until he wishes he were.

I'll have to admit that a lot of the discipline, if you can call it that, is left up to my coaches. I always like to have coaches around me who will chew out anybody who needs it. Coming from a coach, and a coach whose ability they know about and respect, the correction is not so hard to take—and they can even answer back if they dare and not feel too put down.

All the players know the rules and no one spies on them to make sure they obey. Flagrant violations show up without anybody's looking for them. Occasional slips I would overlook anyway, or just pass them off with a hard look. I don't want the guys to get the feeling that I am a Simon Legree or a schoolmaster. They are grownups if they get to the majors and I want them to look and act the part. If a guy shows up around the hotel without a tie, he will be sent back to get one. And nobody in our crew wanders into a hotel dining room in his shirt-sleeves or takes his meal standing up at some quick-and-dirty. This is partly in recognition of the fact that public relations is part of our job—that we want people to think of us as champions and to follow us on that account. But it is also a way of creating self-respect and a sort of *esprit de corps* among the players. A guy who lets himself wander around ragged and tousled may tell himself that he doesn't give a damn what people think of him. But what he really means is that he does not think a hell of a lot of himself. I want my guys to be proud of their club and proud of themselves and glad to belong to a gang of winners.

Another thing that matters a great deal in winning is condition. Condition has a lot to do with attitude, I think, for it requires a real drive to excel and to stay on top. Because it takes hard work and concentration to stay in physical shape. Just playing baseball does not by itself condition a man. He still has to work out, to watch his weight, to get his share of rest, and to practice the moves he may have to make some day in a hurry. And that takes dedication. I know all about that because I am a man who likes good food and drink as well as anybody you ever ran into, and I have to fight off the temptation to overindulge. Maybe I don't have to fight it as I did in my playing days. But I still hold it even.

Then I have some special methods of my own to build strength in the club where it is most needed. I have already talked about a catcher's need to be agile and to be able to get in front of any sort of pitch. Well, I give my catchers plenty of work at stopping tough pitches. I will stand part way to the mound and throw the ball in to the catcher behind the plate, banging it right into the dirt on this side and then on that, making him jump around and dig pitches out until his tongue is pretty near the ground. It happens that my guys eat this up, especially Etchebarren, who will wear me out sooner than I tire him. They know that an ability to stop stuff like that can be crucial in a ball game and they are just as determined as I am to give nothing away to the other side.

The pitchers on our squad as I pointed out get plenty of running, every day, unless they are going to pitch, or have just worked hard the day before. And they don't jog through the outfield the way they may have done in grandpa's day. They *run*. And they sprint. And they sweat. And as a result, they build the strength in their legs that they need to carry them through those brutal midsummer days when the ground is sometimes hard as the sidewalk.

The batters, as I explained, get a lot more bunting practice I think than they would get anywhere else, and this helps them in other ways than in just learning to bunt. When you have to face a pitch that starts about halfway between the mound and the plate, you learn to react *fast*. And above all you learn to keep your eye right on that baseball, without permitting anything to distract you. There is no time to adjust, and you have to pick the ball up immediately or you miss it. I think this helps sharpen a man's batting eye for his regular swing too and gives him more confidence at the plate and better control of his bat.

What I like to see most on my club is the sort of dedication that Frank Robinson displays. Here is a guy who has been in the game for what some men might count a full career. And he has really hit the top too, getting that MVP as a sort of climax to his eleven years in the majors. Yet here he is carrying a loaded bat around with him in his offhours, just to strengthen his arm and shoulder and wrist muscles and make himself into a better hitter. Better than he was in 1966? I don't see how that could be, but Frank is trying it. And I think a lot of youngsters who begin to gripe about having to work too hard can take a lesson from Frank. Here he is, *still* working extra hard and still looking for a way to make himself a little better, and more use to the club. And of course, if he's more valuable to the club, there should be more money in it.

It's not that I want to say that Frank is any more dedicated than other fellows on the club. But he is exceptional because, if anybody might have a reason to rest on past performance it would be Frank. Frank, however has got a glimpse of what it can mean to his family to build the lifelong security that baseball success can bring you, and he has just made up his mind to go after it. Some of the younger players have a hard time getting that view, and a few may even think that natural ability is going to carry them the whole distance.

What happens to championship clubs sometimes is that after they have taken first prize a few times, they begin, without realizing it, to coast a little. Anybody is likely to relax when the prize is in his hands and try to get the enjoyment out of it. But after it has happened a few times, some guys may begin to take victory for granted and either not get themselves into sharp condition, or not give out with that deep-down effort that hurts. This is where the manager comes in again. It is up to him to make those guys see that they are really not bearing down, even if they think they are, and to help them understand what personal goal may be within their reach if they just find the will to punish themselves a bit more.

Because baseball, even when it is fun, does often require that a man punish himself—to get that last bit of reserve strength he needs, or to stay in top condition and be ready when the extra demand comes. As a matter of fact, I think one of the deepest satisfactions in baseball—the thing that makes it the most fun sometimes—is to discover that reserve strength lying there just when you thought you were pooped out, and to discover that you can make those pitches hum even when you are tired, or can get to that ball even when your body tells you to give up on it.

Luis Aparicio is another player who can serve as an example to the young. He too has what might be called a full career behind him, and yet he put in what was undoubtedly his best year in baseball in 1966. And he is still talking about better things ahead. Sometimes it is hard to decide if men like Aparicio and Robinson do better because their clubs are doing better, or if their clubs do well because Frank and Luis are having exceptional years. I think it is a little of both, a sort of interaction that holds the real secret of coming in first. The big guys get off to a good start and they inspire the rest of the club, not just by their example, but by their attitude, by the way they talk it up during the game, by their readiness to help move those runs into scoring position, and of course by their play. Then the momentum of the club begins to carry them, so they develop more confidence, put out that little extra effort, and so provide even more inspiration than they did at the start. A championship team always has a lot of stars on it. And the funny thing is that a championship club always has to have at least one guy playing "over his head"—hitting well above his regular average, throwing harder than ever before, making the plays that no one thought he was capable of. That's how winning can inspire a guy, and how inspiration can feed back to the guys who started it all until you have a club that just refuses to be licked.

Sometimes a club that looks strongest on paper, that has all the high batting averages and the strong pitching, will just be unable to put a string of wins together, while a bunch of just-average guys playing with a nucleus of inspired veterans runs off with the race. You can think of any number of "paper" championships in baseball, who could not take the flag, and a number of "miracle" winners who all played, it seems, far above their ability. The 1967 Red Sox are a prime example of the latter.

Of course, the ability was really there or the plays would not have been made, the hits gathered, or the games pitched. But bringing out that latent ability, making the player dig deep down into himself to find strength he did not know existed—that's what inspiration and dedication and team play can do. The manager can't do it. He can't inspire the club by pep talks and promises. But what he can do is insist on that close cooperation, that devotion to the club, that willingness to give out a little extra rather than let the others down that turns a bunch of good ballplayers into champions.